# WHERE THE BEAR WALKS

## FROM FEAR TO UNDERSTANDING

CHRIS NUNNALLY

ISBN-13: 978-1480198241

Printed by CreateSpace Independent Publishing Platform
Cover design by Nathan Diffee

Printed in the United States

Anniston, AL.

*Dedicated to the mighty grizzly and to all the men and women who who work tirelessly to save him.*

*To Les and Evy Kinnear for opening the door and to Chaik and Killisnoo for showing me what's possible.*

*And in memory of Julie Helgeson and Michele Koons, that their deaths not be in vain and their lives forever remembered.*

# CONTENTS

# ACKNOWLEDGMENTS

Most of the people who deserve recognition for this book are profiled within its pages. I would like to say a special thank you to Doug Peacock, Charlie Russell, and Stephen Stringham for their willingness to patiently answer a plethora of questions and to go above and beyond the call in providing a wealth of information and content review. Thank you also to Doug Seus, Lynn Rogers, Else Poulsen, Casey Anderson, and Nikita Ovsyanikov for going against the grain and showing a side of bears not readily apparent to most.

Thanks also to Katherine Kendall and the Northern Divide Grizzly Bear Project, everyone at BearSaver, Chris Servheen for his comments about the whitebark pine situation, the International Exotic Animal Sanctuary, Jill Robinson, Annemarie Weegenaar, Nicola Field and the entire staff of Animals Asia, Evyn & Nathan Diffee, Sausha Seus, Andrea Peacock, Norbert Rosing, Sue Mansfield, and Allen Piche. And a big thank you to all the readers of my blog, also called "Where the Bear Walks", which helped make the writing of this book possible.

"Unless someone like you cares a whole awful lot, it's not going to get better. It's not."

-Dr. Seuss, The Lorax

"In the end, we will conserve only what we love. We will love only what we understand. We will understand only what we are taught."

-Baba Dioum

"Don't be trapped by dogma – which is living with the results of other people's thinking."

-Steve Jobs

# INTRODUCTION

I love grizzly country. I love hiking, camping, and recreating in grizzly country. In fact, I don't think there is any other place on earth that feels more wild and untamed and for me that's part of the appeal of being out there. But it's also a place where the imagination runs wild, where the rustling of a branch in the wind outside your tent becomes the sound of a prowling beast, where the legions of bear-related horror stories that permeate our society simply will not fade away. Despite how much I've learned over the years, the echoes of those stories still haunt me in those wild places. I think they haunt all of us to some degree. They're ingrained into us, an instinctive fear left over from the days when our ancestors were not masters over the great bear, when they faced him with primitive weapons and their bare hands instead of repeating rifles and shotguns, when we often became easy prey.

Thankfully, those days are long gone, but that primal fear has not abated. Hollywood certainly hasn't helped with that. Neither have sporting magazines with their colorful illustrations of bears tearing helpless hikers into bloody pieces. Bookshelves are lined with volume after volume of sensationalized attack stories while decidedly more educational fare is relegated to near obscurity on internet websites. When the rare attack does occur, the media runs with it, plastering the words "BEAR ATTACK" in screaming headlines. Very seldom is a word given to what caused the attack and never is a story devoted to the thousands of hikers who have peaceful encounters with bears on a daily basis. Is it any wonder then that fear of bears permeates our society to the level of near-paranoia? Certainly bears demand caution and respect, but is such a high degree of fear truly justified?

When I first traveled to Alaska onboard a cruise ship in 2007, a book called *Alaska Bear Tales* caught my eye at a gift shop in Juneau. I couldn't have cared less about bears at the time, so I thought what most tourists no doubt think when confronted with such material: that it would make for good "entertaining" reading from the safety of a cruise ship balcony and not much else. I passed the book by but, when I returned for a more extended stay the following summer, somehow a copy found its way into my hands. If you haven't read the book, you're probably not missing much. Despite some useful information here and there, it consists primarily of blood-spilling, bone-crushing horror stories that make *Jaws* look like *Finding Nemo*. The things that interest me the most about bears – in particular their high intelligence and complex emotions – were brought to my attention in the darkest way possible and I was numbed with horror within only a couple dozen pages. My hiking aspirations were pretty well dashed! Not only did I not want to go into the woods anymore, I didn't even want to leave the house anymore. At night, large dark shapes lumbered up to my bedside. Thus, in the grimmest way possible, my fascination with bears began.

As frightening as the stories were, they didn't keep me out of the woods for very long. What would have been the point of staying in Alaska if they had? Throughout the entirety of that summer and the countless hours of trail time logged, I never encountered a bear and only saw bear sign once. It wasn't long before I started to feel quite foolish.

The fascination didn't end when that summer did. If anything, it had firmly taken hold and was never going to go away. Despite the wealth of more informative material that was available, I was mostly interested in books about bear attacks. I don't know why that particular subject was of such interest to me, but it certainly left me with a very narrow-minded perspective about all things ursine. I often wondered why we didn't just use every bit of available firepower we had and hunt these "killing machines" into extinction. I still hear that opinion expressed now and then, mostly from people who don't live in grizzly country and who have no experience with them, but I'm grateful to see that attitude is not prevalent. And I'm grateful to have found the right people at the right time; people who helped me to develop a better and more informed opinion.

The purpose of this book is to introduce you to those people, those few radicals who have dared to defy dogmatic beliefs in an attempt to show bears for what they really are. In a sense, I'm going to take you on the same journey I've been on; a journey of learning that bears are not the bloodthirsty monsters of horror stories, but surprisingly intelligent and complicated beings not too much unlike us and if ever there were a time when such ideals were needed, it's now.

We're near a critical turning point in the future of the grizzly bear. The planet's life support systems are failing and Yellowstone's grizzlies are ranging far and wide outside of their normal territorial boundaries in search of protein to supplement a rapidly dying source of natural foods, expanding even into human habitations where they have met a wall of human intolerance based on misinformation. Meanwhile, wildlife managers are busy squabbling with each other over who is and who is not an expert, chasing their tails in continual circles, or making unsound decisions about the future of grizzlies, all in the name of a political game. If the species is going to have any hope of survival, attitudes will have to change, outdated dogmas will have to be rethought, and voices that can promulgate change will have to be raised. My hope is that this book, combining the collective work of so many passionate individuals, will help to be an instrument of that change. Bears – particularly grizzlies – are the ultimate symbol of wilderness and wild places and, as an umbrella species, indicators of healthy ecosystems. We cannot afford to lose them.

Grizzly country is not a place for mindless fear. It's a place for solitude and quiet introspection. And if the thought of sharing that place with such a wild and powerful presence increases your heart rate and quickens your pace, then the land is all the richer for it. I know the heightened sense of awareness I feel in grizzly country is something I have never experienced anywhere else and I can't imagine too many more places on earth that could ever replicate it. It's a place where you can truly say that you are alive and "awake". Let's make sure that never changes.

# PART 1:
# A GRISLY HISTORY

# CHAPTER ONE:

## THE GREAT BEAR HOLOCAUST

It's hard to believe today that an estimated 100,000 grizzlies once roamed North America, roughly 10,000 of those in Southern California alone. From the Mexican Rockies through the Southwestern deserts, across the vast Great Plains to the rugged coastline of the Pacific states, grizzlies that sometimes topped out over 1,000 pounds prowled the landscape. These were the days before the westward expansion, before the arrival of the white man and the European, when the West was still wild and untamed.

It's telling that the conflict between the two species did not really begin until the white man came, bringing with him the American penchant to dominate and subdue all that stands before him. The Native Americans lived alongside the grizzly with few problems. In fact, many tribes revered the bears, giving them names such as "grandfather" and "elder brother", due to the many similar characteristics the grizzlies shared with man. To some, they were gods and creation legends centering around the grizzly were told and passed down (they viewed the black bear as cowardly due to its timid nature and did not consider them to be real bears), while others believed that women could morph into grizzlies. Still others believed their ancestors were reincarnated as bears and treated them with great reverence and respect. The tribes that hunted the grizzly did so as a rite of passage or a spiritual experience; a task not to be taken lightly.

The long-standing peace between man and bear ended abruptly in 1804 when Lewis and Clark began their famous expedition west. Having no knowledge of the great bears, the men often surprised them at close range, foolishly chased them, or otherwise provoked the animals into attacking. The explorers were quick to use their weapons, marveling at how difficult the animals were to kill. Some bears fell under no less than eight rifle balls, prompting the men to write of the unnaturally aggressive temperament of the beasts. In truth, that extreme aggression was caused by the ineffectiveness of their primitive weapons to do little more than cause maddening pain.

There is no doubt that Lewis and Clark contributed heavily to science (the discovery of the grizzly, ironically, is considered to be one of their greatest*), and to the birth of our civilization, but there can also be no doubt that they were the first to paint the grizzly bear in an unfavorable light. When their published journals became popular in 1825, the image of the grizzly as North America's most fearsome beast was subsequently burned into the minds of the public. As told around thousands of campfires and printed in as many books, Lewis and Clark's misunderstanding of the grizzly's powerful build, curious nature, and hair-trigger defenses became so further embellished that, when the westward expansion finally began, along with it came an assortment of guns and traps suitable enough to take on this sinister brute.

The killing began in California. With the westward flow of humanity, cattle inevitably followed, soon becoming a big business. As early as the late 1830's, large tracts of prime grizzly habitat were being converted to pasture and farmland. With the advent of large-caliber weapons and repeating rifles, and the fear that cattle would make easy pickings for the large bears, ranchers and farmers hired professional hunters to exterminate grizzlies on their land and some of these hunters were rumored to have killed as many as 200 bears in one year's time.

Those grizzlies unlucky enough to fall before the bullets were taken alive for use in public grudge matches against 2,000 pound Spanish bulls. More often than not, the bears would actually shy away from the bulls, attempting to dig a hole to hide in. But when the bull struck and blood was drawn, the confrontation usually ended quickly. The battered and bleeding grizzly would then be subjected to round after round of the fights until it finally succumbed to death, to the great delight of bloodthirsty spectators.

Eventually public outcry against bear/bull fights finally put an end to the barbaric sport, but there was never to be any such outcry against the mass slaughter that was occurring and the killing continued until every last grizzly had been exterminated from the state of California.

In the late 1870's, large cattle ranches laid claim to open grasslands in the West and immediately ran into wildlife problems. While true predators like wolves and mountain lions were responsible for most of the stock killing, it was the grizzly that got most of the blame. Bears are actually very inefficient predators and usually resort to scavenging and feeding on carcasses left behind by other animals. When a rancher would go in search of a cattle carcass, he would find a grizzly feeding on it and naturally assume the bear must have been the killer. As it was in California, professional hunters were hired to shoot grizzlies on sight and some of these men were unspeakably cruel in their practices.

*It was actually Spanish explorers in the 1500's who should be given this credit.

James "Bear" Moore was one of the most deranged. His face half mangled from a bear he had wounded, he specialized in trapping grizzlies inside a small cabin structure and then would wreak his own personal vengeance by impaling them for hours with white-hot iron rods. When he tired of the torture, he would shoot the hapless animals. Others would corner grizzlies in culvert traps, douse them with gasoline, and light them on fire.

As the wildlife war raged on, a more effective solution was devised: strychnine. Believed to be a quick and painless death, this slow-acting poison actually causes severe muscle spasms and it can take up to half an hour for its victim to finally die. Stocked in mercantile stores throughout the West, this lethal concoction would be the grizzly's final downfall. Even the newly-created U.S. Forest Service, more concerned with appeasing ranchers than with protecting wildlife, joined in on the poisoning campaign. Then the U.S. Congress created PARC, the Predatory Animal and Rodent Control Division of the Department of Agriculture, and set in motion a "final solution" for predator control. Massive doses of strychnine and strychnine-laced beef were spread across the countryside by hundreds of government agents.

And no one said a word. No government employees or Forest Service rangers or ranchers or civilians ever questioned what was being done. They did their jobs and reaped the monetary rewards for their silence.

The last grizzly in Texas fell in 1890, then in South Dakota in 1897. The grizzly was declared extinct in Mexico in 1920, then California – once one of the largest strongholds for the great bear – in 1922. Utah's last was killed in 1923, Oregon's in 1931 and Washington's in 1936. New Mexico lost its last in 1933 and Arizona followed in 1939. The final holdout was a female in the San Juan Mountains of Colorado, killed in 1952. A species a hundred thousand strong had been reduced to only a few hundred.

The remaining survivors fled into the high mountains of Yellowstone and Glacier National Parks in an attempt to escape the bounties and the bloodshed and today those reserves are the last enclaves of the North American grizzly outside of Canada and Alaska. The establishment of the parks is probably all that stopped the holocaust from following them until there were none left. Now those survivors are waiting. Waiting for a change. Waiting for a day when they're once again free to roam, when these last strongholds are not all they have left.

Unfortunately, the legend of the killer bear is still with us. The days of Lewis and Clark have left us with that inaccurate and misinformed idea and we have yet to let go of it. To this day, fierce battles are waged over the future of the grizzly and what the bear is actually worth. There are a disturbing number who feel that the mass extermination should be re-implemented and should continue until the species is extinct. Fortunately, their voices are not the loudest and there are even more individuals who are standing on the frontlines every day, trying to save what's left of these bears and trying to change the world's perception of them.

With the eradication of the plains grizzly, the roaring gunfire that echoed throughout the western states finally faded to a grim silence. But silence was meant to be broken. It was misguided fear of the grizzly that nearly destroyed him and, in the decades that followed, the bear was completely taken for granted in Glacier National Park. Garbage dumps were publicly opened for bear feeding shows, trash was dumped in culverts and ditches behind alpine chalets and, running underneath it all, was the equally misguided belief that the great bears were not really dangerous...

Present and historic grizzly bear distribution.

# CHAPTER TWO:

## THE NIGHT OF THE GRIZZLIES

In August 1967, this lethal combination of negligence and poor management practices came together in an unprecedented perfect storm that claimed the lives of the most innocent victims.

On August 12th, 19-year-old Julie Helgeson, a lovely girl with brown hair and blue eyes, hiked into Granite Park Chalet with her boyfriend Roy Ducat. Roy and Julie were both employees at East Glacier Lodge and had been spending each weekend of their summer hiking and exploring the park. Julie, described by her father as a "beautiful, bubbling girl", relished any opportunity to get into the woods and surround herself with the deep peace of nature. A college sophomore who was enormously well-liked by her peers back home in Minnesota, Julie had just said good-bye to her parents a few days before. They had spent two days in the park visiting their daughter, unknowingly for the last time.

Roy and Julie had planned to stay in the chalet that night, so they didn't give much thought to the fact that the area was the site of one of the park's bear feeding shows. Unfortunately, the chalet was full and they were forced to spend the night in a makeshift campground 500 yards down the hillside. With no tents, the young couple rolled out their sleeping bags for a night under the stars, not knowing that a bear trail running from the woods to the dump site at the chalet passed very near to the campground.

Simultaneously, nine miles away in almost a straight shot over the top of 8,987 foot Heaven's Peak, 19-year-old Michele Koons and a group of her friends were setting up camp on the shore of Trout Lake. A sophomore from San Diego, Michele was equally well-liked and respected. Voted "Most Likely to Succeed" by her classmates, Michele had a bright smile and a warm welcome for anyone she met. She and her companions Paul Dunn (who, chillingly, was also close friends with Roy and Julie and had originally intended to accompany them to Granite Park before opting for Trout Lake), Ray Noseck, Ron Noseck, and Denise Huckle had already been paid a visit by a bold and ragged-looking bear, making for an uncomfortable evening around the fire.

One doesn't have to read very many books about bears before hearing of Julie Helgeson and Michele Koons. Of all the attacks that have been documented, theirs is the one that seems to stand out the most and that people most want to remember. While a large part of that is no doubt due to the almost impossible to believe circumstances of the incident, another part can be attributed to the girls themselves.

When I first read of their story, it was a one-paragraph summary in *Alaska Bear Tales* that did not even mention the girls by name. Even so, I was struck by something deep and immediately wanted to know who these people were and what had happened to them. It was Jack Olsen's extraordinarily detailed book *Night of the Grizzlies* that made me realize the deep, ineffable bond I felt with Julie and Michele, as if I somehow knew them, even though I never could have. The equally well-done documentary *Glacier Park's Night of the Grizzlies* never fails to choke me up no matter how many times I see it. According to e-mails I've received from my blog readers and the number of tributes I've seen, I'm not alone in these feelings.

This inexplicable connection with these two young women stayed with me and haunted me over the years until I realized that I needed to visit the attack sites in Glacier National Park in order to pay my own respects. I finally was able to do so in August 2012, on the 45th anniversary of their deaths.

The tragedy of that night began shortly after midnight on August 13th, 1967. Roy Ducat was woken from a deep sleep by Julie whispering "play dead." They both remained perfectly still but the bear that stood over them, sniffing and investigating, struck anyway. It knocked Roy from his sleeping bag with one blow and stood on his back, biting into his shoulder and arm. Somehow he managed to stay still and the bear turned its attack on Julie. Numbed with shock, Roy remembered hearing the snap of bones and Julie could be silent no longer. She screamed and those screams slowly faded as she was drug away into the night.

His arm hanging bloody and torn, Roy mustered everything he could and ran back to the chalet for help. As the overnight occupants were roused by the commotion and tried to process what was happening, Roy tried to push away those who came to his aid, pleading with them to leave him and go find Julie. Seasonal ranger Joan Devereaux, who had led a group of hikers into the chalet earlier that day, radioed headquarters and requested a helicopter with medical supplies. Perhaps no coincidence, a surgeon, Dr. Lipinski, was staying in the chalet that night. He tended to Roy's wounds and prepared him for evacuation on the helicopter.

Meanwhile, the painful decision was made to leave Julie alone in the dark until the helicopter arrived with armed backup. This was Devereaux's first command situation and with the general lack of knowledge available about bears at the time, she felt the situation was too dangerous. For all anyone knew, a crazed grizzly could – and *would* – attack and kill a rescue party of a dozen or more people. Some of the chalet's occupants challenged that decision and still feel today that it was the wrong move and that the decision contributed to Julie's death.

Easily the more heartbreaking of the two attacks, Julie spent more than two hours lying on that hillside in the dark, alone and injured, wondering if the bear was going to come back for her. Standing outside Granite Park Chalet 45 years later, I can't begin to imagine the terror she must have felt on that moonless night.

After the helicopter arrived with an armed ranger and medical supplies, Roy was airlifted to a hospital in Kalispell and a search party was finally formed to go after Julie. Steve Pierre, an Indian with honed tracking skills, followed droplets of blood on blades of grass until they led him right to Julie. Severely mauled, she was hoisted onto a makeshift stretcher and carried back to the chalet where a dining room table was converted into a hospital bed. Dr. Lipinski examined Julie's wounds and declared the situation grave. Too much time had passed and too much blood lost. Her veins were collapsing and one lung was punctured from where the bear had apparently picked her up in its mouth and carried her.

Dr. Lipinski was finally able to find an uncollapsed vein and inserted an IV drip. Aside from keeping her comfortable, there was nothing more they could do. Father Tom Connolly, a priest who had hiked in the previous day with Steve Pierre, baptized her, gave her Last Rites, and said the Lord's Prayer over her. Amazingly, Julie quietly followed along. Then she took her last breath, closed her eyes, and died at 4:12 A.M., more than two hours after she had been rescued. Standing in the chalet's dining room 45 years later, I'm overwhelmed by the deepest feeling of peace I've ever experienced.

\*\*\*\*

At 4:30 A.M., eighteen minutes after Julie's death, the odd malnourished bear returned to the campsite at Trout Lake. Paul Dunn awoke to see the animal standing over him. It bit into his sleeping bag, tearing his shirt in the process. Paul bolted from his sleeping bag and ran for a nearby tree, screaming for the others to do the same. The bear, startled by the sudden movement, temporarily retreated into the woods and then returned to the camp. One by one, the others ran for trees…except for Michele Koons, who

Author's photo of Granite Park Chalet in August 2012, 45 years after the death of Julie Helgeson.

was trapped in her sleeping bag, unable to get the zipper down. Fixated on her desperate movements, the bear grabbed Michele and the bag in its mouth. "He's got my arm!" She cried. "Oh my God, I'm dead!" She never made another sound, her death more mercifully swift than Julie's had been.

The others remained in their trees in shock until daylight, and then hurried back over steep Howe Ridge to the ranger station at Lake McDonald. In a frenzied panic, they all simultaneously told their story. Knowing that a bear had been hanging around the Lake McDonald area and had reportedly been behaving very erratically, the ranger asked the kids to show him where the attack had occurred. In the woods, not far from the Trout Lake campground, they found Michele's remains, clearly the victim of a rare predatory attack.

The campground is no longer in use today and has not been used since that night. Hiking over Howe Ridge on August 13th, 2012, I can't help but marvel at how the area has changed. The massive fires of 2003 have devastated the Lake McDonald side of the ridge, leaving me very little shade from the pounding sun and the sweltering 95 degree heat. The foliage on either side of the very narrow trail, however, is coming back with a vengeance. It's high, thick, and chock full of berries. This is prime grizzly habitat, yet I'm feeling eerily calm and detached, as if in a state of heightened awareness. I clap my hands, call out "hey, bear" while approaching the numerous blind corners, and occasionally snap big sticks, sending small animals scurrying in every direction. The hind foot print of a large bear is pressed firmly into the mud in the center of the trail.

Standing on the shore of the lake, I can only guess where the campsite was based on the knowledge that I have of the incident. There is no profound spiritual revelation now that I'm here and I'm not sure I expected there to be one. Just the same sense of overwhelming peace and personal closure that I felt the day before at Granite Park Chalet. As with the chalet, it was with sadness that I began the hike out of Trout Lake, but I did so with the knowledge that I will return here again someday.

\*\*\*\*

The Trout Lake bear was killed a day later by rangers at Arrow Lake. An autopsy revealed a ball of blonde hair in its stomach, leaving no doubt as to the animal's guilt. At Granite Park Chalet, finding the killer was not so easy. Several bears were shot and killed, all individuals that routinely fed at the chalet's garbage dump. None of them could be linked to Julie's death. Then rangers killed a sow with cubs and found dried blood caked between her claws. Samples of the blood were sent away for analysis and it was found to be non-human in origin. Even so, the Park Service declared that it had bagged the killer bear. But had they or was the guilty party long gone? Considering that bears can cover great distances in short periods of time, sometimes traversing hundreds of miles in a day, it's perfectly conceivable that the bear could have been well out of the area by the time the bullets started flying. Some even believe that the bear that attacked Julie was the same bear that killed Michele. While the distance of 9 miles and the time gap of 4 hours are certainly doable for a bear, close analysis of the incident reveals that the female was the most likely culprit.

The attack on Julie Helgeson seemed to fit the pattern of defensive behavior. Julie and Roy were curled up in their sleeping bags, certainly posing no threat. But the sow had cubs and a mother grizzly is a highly dangerous and often unstable creature. Understandable when one considers the threat that male bears pose to young cubs. After the sow was killed, rangers found that one of her paw pads was hanging by a flap of skin, a mysterious injury that would have caused intense, nagging pain, provoking not only a bad attitude but possibly some form of growing derangement.

Apparently, Roy and Julie simply found themselves with the wrong bear at the wrong time. With the cubs and the injury that no doubt made walking an agonizing chore, the bear likely startled easily and attacked blindly. The fact that no human remains were found in the stomach and that Julie was left alone and alive for two hours without the bear coming back for her suggest that the attack was not predatory in nature.

It was a very different story with the Trout Lake bear. Harassing visitors at nearby Kelly's Camp, the bear had been reported to be exhibiting signs of what may have been mental illness. It was also thin and haggard, a bear that had not been getting enough to eat; a bear that rangers should have taken more responsibility in recognizing as a potential threat. The fact that the bear had entered the campsite a few hours before Michele's death would seem to rule out its involvement in Julie's.

The story of these tragic killings spread across the nation like wildfire. Debates raged about what may have caused the attacks and theories ranging from madness caused by lightning storms and wildfires to bloodlust triggered by the girls' menstrual cycles were thrown about. So wild and so pervasive were some of the theories that no one could see that maybe the answer was simply negligence (and no small amount of bad luck) on behalf of the Park Service. Once again, anti-bear sentiment began to grow. Questions were asked: "Why do we need bears?", "What good are they?", and "Why don't we just get rid of them and make our parks safe for everyone?" Even Jack Olsen, in his 1969 book on the attacks, lamented that this incident may finally mark the end of the great and mighty grizzly.

# THE NIGHT OF THE GRIZZLIES

But it wasn't in Glacier where the killing began. It was almost 400 miles to the south, in Yellowstone National Park.

****

Twin brothers John and Frank Craighead began studying grizzly bears in Yellowstone in 1959. Focusing on several generations of grizzlies over a period of thirteen years, the Craighead's pioneered the now often-used technique of radio-collaring bears and tracking their movements. In a scientific study that would become the standard by which all others would be judged, the Craighead's touched on every aspect of grizzly bear life: social interactions, mating, feeding, denning habits, etc., etc., forming the picture of the grizzly and its world that we now know today.

The Craighead's benefitted the park and its bears in many other ways as well, instructing and assisting park rangers and using their expertise at trapping, tracking, and releasing to perform the risky task of capturing and relocating bears that threatened campgrounds. While a few employees of the Park Service inevitably viewed their work as an intrusion, most were grateful for their insights and contributions and, in 1962, the park requested that the brothers draw up a list of management recommendations for handling the bear population. Unfortunately, the fields of wildlife research and wildlife management are, and have always been, uneasy bedfellows, something that would become apparent to the Craighead's in the very near future.

In 1963, a system of "natural guidelines" was proposed that essentially allowed for nature to take care of itself: let wildfires burn out of control, let the animals get wiped out by epidemics, let the grizzlies starve when their numbers exceeded their habitat's carrying capacity. The park approved of the plan and the following year, the Craighead's management ideas were rescinded and they were assigned to strictly research.

As in Glacier, Yellowstone National Park also drew a large number of tourists to the garbage dumps for daily bear feeding shows. Some tourists even stopped to feed the hungry black bears that stood by the roadsides, begging for a handout. One man smeared honey on his young daughter's face, hoping to snap a picture of a bear licking her. The deaths of Julie Helgeson and Michele Koons in 1967 sent just as many shockwaves rippling through Yellowstone as it did in Glacier, leaving park managers in a panic, fearing that they may soon see similar fatalities.

Having spent countless hours tracking and monitoring a number of bears that regularly fed at the dumps, the Craighead's gathered evidence that these bears did not lead adverse lives because of the presence of garbage; in fact, they found that the bears still functioned as fully wild animals when they were away from the dumps, foraging for natural foods and generally ignoring humans rather than associating them with food. They advised the Park Service to gradually close the dumps and slowly wean the bears off of the garbage, warning that an abrupt closure could have the opposite effect, sending the bears into a panic. Ignoring their evidence and advice, park managers insisted the dumps be closed quickly and immediately.

Tragically, the Craighead's were dead on with their prediction. The sudden loss of such a major food source sent the bears into a panic and the number of bear/human encounters in the campgrounds began to skyrocket, with some individual animals developing predatory behavior. According to records kept by Frank, 84 control actions were taken against bears by the Park Service in 1968, more than double what it had been the previous year, but the park managers themselves only kept record of 24 of these actions, advising their rangers to remove the bears but keep it quiet.

In their 1968 annual progress report, the Craighead's openly criticized the park's management plan, criticism that made its way to the highest levels of Washington, where it was not warmly received. Shortly thereafter, the abandoned mess hall Frank and John had been granted permission to use as a research station and living quarters was burned and bulldozed to the ground. The official explanation for this given to the Craighead's was that it was done in preparation for the park's upcoming centennial celebration in 1972, but they denied the brothers use of any other vacant buildings and refused to allow their participation in any further capture and relocation of bears. This would only be the first of many spiteful acts that would be thrown in the faces of bear advocates and researchers in the coming years, contention that still exists to this day because of that tragic night in 1967.

In 1971, when Frank asked to see complete records of all relocation and control actions taken since the dump closures, he was denied. Later the Park Service would openly criticize the Craighead's, claiming the brothers had not been supplying them with recent data, yet the Craighead's contend that each time they handed in reports, the papers were promptly handed right back. The final death blow came when the Park Service stipulated that all publications or comments made by the brothers pertaining to Yellowstone's grizzlies and the park's management of them be approved in advance by the director of the U.S. Fish and Wildlife Service and that that man in turn get the approval of the director of the National Park Service before one word could be printed. The Craighead's, their academic freedom effectively taken away, refused to sign the agreement. The work was over.

# THE NIGHT OF THE GRIZZLIES

The trouble, on the other hand, was just beginning. Fatalities attributed to the improperly weaned bears began to occur, leading to the extermination of forty to fifty grizzlies a year. Frank predicted that if those management practices were to continue, the grizzly would be wiped out by 1990. He noted that in a two-year period, 1970-1972, the population had been cut in half, leaving only an estimated 100 individuals surviving in the park. The repercussions of the infamous Night of the Grizzlies were threatening to bring about the end of the grizzlies.

The establishment of the Endangered Species Act in 1973 finally put an end to the killing, otherwise the grizzly may very well have been wiped out as Frank predicted. Today, thanks to these Federal protections, there are now estimated to be between 1,400 and 1,600 grizzlies inhabiting the Lower 48 tier of North America and the population is stable and thriving.

The deaths of Julie and Michele were a deep loss to those who knew them – and to many who didn't – but have also done more to influence bear management and politics than any other documented incident. It's the reason why park policies today are so much stricter. It's the reason why bear warnings are emphasized to an almost exaggerated extent. It's part of the reason why bear spray was invented and why hikers are so much safer in grizzly country now than they were before (as of this writing, there has not been a fatality attributed to bear attack in Glacier National Park in 15 years). It's the reason why such passionate, even venomous, debate rages in the halls of wildlife management. It's the reason why the grizzly was once again almost exterminated, why they were granted federal protections, and why they thrive in abundance now. The repercussions of that night continue to be felt today and that at least gives some meaning to the loss of such bright, young lives.

I wonder about Julie and Michele, though. I wonder, if they could see all that's been brought about in the wake of their deaths – the better education, safer management practices, and the salvation of an animal that once seemed doomed to extinction, - would they feel those deaths were worth it? I don't know. But I do hope they would understand that they did not die in vain.

# CHAPTER THREE:

## THE PUBLIC BATTLES

Under the auspices of the Endangered Species Act, the U.S. Fish and Wildlife Service established the following grizzly bear recovery zones:

- The Greater Yellowstone Ecosystem (GYE) in northwest Wyoming, eastern Idaho, and southwest Montana, comprising 9,200 square miles with more than 580 bears.

- The Northern Continental Divide Ecosystem (NCDE) of north-central Montana, encompassing Glacier National Park and covering more than 9,600 square miles with more than 400 bears.

- The North Cascades area in north-central Washington, comprising 9,500 square miles and less than 20 grizzlies.

- The Selkirk Mountains of northern Idaho, northeast Washington, and southeast British Columbia, covering 2,200 square miles with about 40-50 bears.

- The Cabinet Yaak area of northwest Montana and northern Idaho, comprising 2,600 square miles with approximately 30-40 bears.

An additional recovery area was established in the Bitterroot Mountains of east-central Idaho and western Montana, covering 5,600 square miles. It is believed that this area does not contain grizzlies and is thus a prime choice for possible reintroduction. The San Juan Mountains of Colorado have also been identified as a potential recovery zone with some already believing that the great bear still inhabits the area in small numbers.

Many critics argue that the recovery zones, while federally managed and mostly roadless, are too small and ignore bear populations outside of those areas. Without safe corridors linking the zones together, the bears are isolated in these small islands, genetically cut off from individuals in other habitats. Thus, conservation organizations are working feverishly on what they call Y2Y, Yukon to Yellowstone, an open corridor of sustainable habitat linking grizzly recovery areas from the Yukon Territory to Yellowstone National Park. It's still only a dream but a number of passionate individuals believe that one day it will be made reality and, with any luck, that day will come soon.

In the Yellowstone Ecosystem, the whitebark pine, its nuts a favored food of grizzlies and a source of much-needed late season protein, is slowly dying out as a result of a growing pine beetle infestation (see chapter twelve for more info). The grizzly is a very adaptable animal and without the necessary corridors to travel from one island habitat to another, they are now ranging far and wide outside of their normal territory in search of supplemental protein and entering human habitations, much to the horror of the general public. This, unsurprisingly, has refueled much of the same anti-bear sentiment that has existed in one form or another since the 1800's.

The Wind River Range in Wyoming is some of the best bear habitat out there but after Fremont County declared the grizzly a "socially unacceptable species", citing fear of public maulings and deaths, the animals have not been allowed to go there. Likewise, Idaho Representative Helen Chenoweth compared bringing grizzlies into the Bitterroots to "introducing sharks at the beach." Then Senator Steve Symms (R-Idaho) proclaimed that grizzlies are only valuable because they "make excellent rugs."

Gov. Dirk Kempthorne, who went on to become Interior Secretary under George W. Bush (who temporarily, and fraudulently, removed the Yellowstone grizzly from Federal protections in 2007, despite the protests of his own biologists), said that grizzlies were nothing more than "massive, flesh-eating carnivores" and that any reintroduction plan "could be the first land management plan in history likely to result in injury or death to members of the public."

That public has been the most vicious responder. At a public meeting in Okanogan, Washington, wildlife biologist Doug Zimmer was sent to preside over a presentation about grizzly reintroduction into the Cascade Mountains. It was at one of these meetings that he found himself confronted by an elderly woman: 'So you're one of those bastards in favor of grizzly bears!" She railed and cursed at him, telling him that he would be responsible for the death of her grandchildren, then she promptly spat on him. By the end of the evening, Zimmer had received *nine* death threats, including one from a man who vowed to be waiting outside the building with a gun to kill Zimmer, a threat that fortunately proved to be only a bluff.

Biologists and grizzly recovery coordinators scoff at such paranoid overreactions. They know that a bear's diet is composed of 80-90% plants, vegetation, and insects and that they will not kill schoolchildren at bus stops and break into houses to rip people out of their beds. Those who live in grizzly country understand this and they make up the largest number of those who are in favor of grizzly recovery, while those who don't live around bears or any other type of wildlife tend to hold the view that wild animals are hyper-dangerous serial killers in fur coats.

Maybe it's this line of thinking that has caused so many government and wildlife agencies to persist in brushing aside the issue of grizzly recovery, particularly in the Cascades. Jon Almack, project leader for the North Cascades Grizzly Evaluation, said that he personally observed a "strategy within the Washington Department of Fish and Wildlife to deny, discount, and dismiss the evidence about Cascades grizzlies…I was told to go as slow as I possibly could."

Perhaps wildlife managers know that if they continue to deny the most irrefutable of evidence that grizzlies exist in the Cascades*, they can delay recovery for as long as possible, maybe even until there is no longer a species left to recover. The Interagency Grizzly Bear Committee now estimates that it could take as long as 200 years to restore grizzlies to the Cascades.

This is a shocking prospect! The idea that wildlife managers, who are supposed to be working towards the survival of threatened species, would instead be stalling the issue until it's too late, is difficult to fathom, but it's exactly the reason why we need the people who are profiled in the next section and why we need to start listening to them. Through their work, they are trying to show that sharing the land with bears is a blessing, not a curse, and that they do not deserve the reputation we've forced upon them. That's the goal we're working towards, at least, but it seems a long road getting there.

---

*In 2011, a clear photograph of a grizzly bear was taken in the North Cascades by a hiker, leaving their presence in the area no longer in dispute.

# PART 2:
# THE BEAR PEOPLE

# CHAPTER FOUR:

## MAN'S BEST FRIEND?

During those early days when bear attack literature made up the bulk of my education, Doug Seus was the first individual whose work inspired me to consider other possibilities. Stationed in Heber City, Utah, Seus is considered to be the "Moses of animal trainers" and the best bear trainer in the world. He may also be one of the foremost experts on bear behavior and psychology.

Interested in animals from a young age (he jokes his father benched him in Little League for trying to catch butterflies), his dream was to own and raise a Kodiak grizzly bear, one of the largest bears on earth, a distinction shared only with the polar bear. Family and friends didn't understand and tried to talk Doug out of this unthinkable notion, insisting that he and his wife Lynne should get real jobs. But Doug didn't want a real job; he wanted a Kodiak.

In 1977, he and Lynne obtained a bear permit and a zoo placed them with a newborn Kodiak who had barely even opened his eyes. Working intensively with the cub, named Bart (pictured above as an adult), Doug taught him patience and how to cope with the stresses of the human world, all the while grooming the little tyke for a life in front of the camera.

In the two decades that followed, Bart the Bear would become the most famous animal actor since Lassie. Trained to show emotion and characterization, Bart was met with instant accolades and an impressive career. He was humorous in *The Great Outdoors*, emotional in *The Bear*, and terrifying in *The Edge*, leaving many of his human co-stars in awe not only of his ability to perform but of the strict obedience he displayed to Doug. Bart finally made it to the Academy Awards in 1998 as part of a tribute to animal actors.

The bond established between Doug and Bart throughout the 23 years they spent together was deeper than friendship, deeper than companionship. "He was my soulmate," Doug says of Bart. It was a relationship that many could not have imagined possible between man and bear. Despite Bart's tragic death from cancer in 2000, Doug has continued his work with Tank, Little Bart, and Honey-Bump, who have appeared in *Dr. Dolittle 2* (this, *The Bear*, and *The Edge*, in my eyes, represent animal training at its finest), *Without a Paddle, Into the Wild, Zookeeper*, and the upcoming *Red Machine*.

Outside of these movies, my exposure to Doug and his work came through a YouTube video called "The Legacy of Bart the Bear", produced by Vital Ground, a conservation organization started by Doug and Lynne in 1990 to buy back private land for usage as grizzly bear habitat. As I watched Doug running Little Bart and Honey-Bump through their training exercises, playing and romping with them like big dogs, I was stunned. I couldn't understand how someone could work so closely and so safely with such a "vicious creature", but that video lingered with me more than the horror stories did. Bears now seemed to me to be a walking contradiction, and I needed to know how something like this could be possible.

It would be two more years before I found my answer.

## FORTRESS OF THE BEAR

In 2002, Les Kinnear, a resident of Sitka, Alaska and a former hunting and fishing guide, had tired of picking up the local paper and reading about brown bear cubs that were left orphaned after their mothers had been shot, usually after getting into trouble with people and their food. These cubs, with no mother to protect and teach them, stood little chance of surviving on their own. Les felt that someone should take the initiative and do something to help give those cubs a chance at life. His wife Evy asked simply "When do we start?"

Thus began an intensive five-year endeavor to make the dream a reality. Les and Evy acquired two water treatment tanks left abandoned for nine years on an old pulp mill site and began the long process of detoxing the tanks and removing three hundred tons of leftover materials. All that scrap metal was replaced with dirt, sod, grass, rocks, and trees. A swimming pool was added and a nearby mountain stream diverted to flow into the enclosure, creating a naturally filtering fresh water system.

Finally, in 2007, the long years of hard, grueling work paid off when the Alaska Department of Fish and Game granted the Kinnear's their bear permit. No one could have known how fortuitous the timing was.

41 miles away near Angoon on Admiralty Island (called "Kootznoowoo" – fortress of the bears – by the native Tlingits), a gunshot rang out, leaving dead the female brown bear who was trying to obtain food for her three malnourished cubs at Whaler's Cove Lodge. Two of the cubs, both males, were rescued and taken to Sitka, just eight days after Les and Evy had obtained their permit. The third cub, a female, was lost.

The two brothers, named Killisnoo (kills-new) and Chaik (shy-eek) after an old Indian village and a sheltered inlet near where they were found, began the long process of acclimating to their new environment and their new, upright parents. Now, six years later, they are healthy, strong, weighing over 1,000 pounds each, and are two of the most sociable bears in captivity anywhere.

In the summer of 2010, I was invited to Sitka and given the opportunity to work up close with Chaik and Killisnoo and further my own education on the subject. The insights I gained into bear behavior were astounding and have influenced my writings ever since. Face to face with the mind and soul of the bear, the mysterious puzzle pieces that make up bear training and Doug Seus' profound relationship with his grizzly family finally came together for me.

A common misconception about bears is that they belong to the pig family, which is partly due to the equally common misconception that they will and do eat anything and everything they find, and partly because of the usage of the terms "boar" and "sow" to identify male and female bears. It is probable that those terms were used for bears long before they were adopted for pigs due to the word "boar" being derived from the word "bear". In actuality, though, bears are more closely related to dogs, the Ursidae and Canidae families both being part of the Caniformia branch of the order Carnivora. In simpler language, this means that bears share many of the same qualities as man's best friend, including a deep sense of loyalty once a bond has been effectively established. This is a big part of how people such as Les and Doug are able to do what they do with their bears.

At the Fortress, daily training exercises are used to establish and maintain a rapport between the bears and their keepers. Working through a barrier, trainers teach the bears simple commands that re-enforce natural behaviors, with white grapes offered as reward. With a verbal command and hand signal, the bears will open their mouths so that keepers can examine their gums and teeth, extend their paws through an opening in the barrier, place the top of their heads flat against the barrier (Chaik in particular enjoys getting his head scratched while in this position), stand, sit, lie down, and roll over. On occasion, Chaik will show affection by licking his keeper's face when a training session is over.

Beginning this kind of work with bears at a very young age is critical to its success*, as that will ensure that the cub will imprint on its human keeper as a mother, a bond the bear will carry throughout its life. Some feel that a cub over the age of four months is too feral to be tamed but Killisnoo and Chaik, having arrived at Fortress at 7 and 9 months respectively, would seem to disprove that notion.

## INTELLIGENCE

When you think of the most intelligent non-human animals on earth, what comes to mind? Dolphins, whales, and primates obviously, but probably not bears. With their reputation as slow, lumbering, garbage cans, many people regard them as being similar in intelligence to herds of cattle. In truth, bears are equal in intelligence to the main three listed above, and a few biologists have even gone so far as to declare some bears as having the mental faculties of a 4-year-old child.

While some of the more extreme environmentalists oppose the practice of keeping bears in captivity, I feel that, if well cared for and provided with a thoroughly enriching environment, captive bears can offer the best insights into their own minds and offer new ideas about how to deal with and approach their wild cousins. Chaik and Killisnoo provide those insights on a daily basis.

On one occasion, during the summer of 2010, Chaik was behaving aggressively towards his brother, robbing him of his enrichment toys, and not permitting him to have any fun. Marie, our summer intern, and I found Killisnoo inside the training room, lying against the wall with his head down. He extended his paw through the barrier, gently curled his claws around Marie's fingers, and held on tightly. It was that moment that I realized what a great capacity for emotion these animals possess.

---

*Needless to say that getting the animals fixed at a certain point also helps to curb aggression and competition.

One of the most remarkable things I witnessed that summer is the quiet and respectful way that the brothers behave when face to face with their human keepers. One of my earliest memories is visiting a Birmingham, Alabama zoo as a young child and seeing a large gorilla fly into a rampage. Roaring and pounding on the glass of his exhibit, the glass rippling like waves, people were running and screaming in every direction. That inevitably colored my thinking of how wild animals would behave in a captive environment, and I was initially nervous about working with the bears up close, fearing that I would give the wrong command or confuse hand signals and they would react aggressively, roaring and pounding the bars that separated me from them. Now I look back at that and laugh. If anything, Chaik and Killisnoo were the epitome of courtesy and respect.

Entering the training room for a session – one would only have to call them by name or bang on the bars to bring them running – they would playfully wrestle and spar with each other until reaching the entrance to the den area, then the behavior would instantly cease and they would approach the keeper slowly and deliberately, allowing every movement they made to be clearly seen, as if intentionally trying not to make us feel nervous or intimidated. "No horsing around" seemed to be the unspoken agreement between them when they were up close and personal with us. On the days when we cleaned out their den area, they would sit at the gate, side by side like two bookends, and quietly watch, never losing patience or becoming unruly, until the work was done and they were allowed to enter. During training sessions, we would feed them by hand and they would gently pluck the sweet treats from our fingers using only their lips, skin and teeth never once making contact. They were not trained or taught to be this respectful; they did it of their own choosing, a natural response to the bond that had been established.

I was and still am amazed by this behavior. Karen Cain from the Anchorage Zoo came to visit in the fall of 2010 and said they were the most obedient and socialized bears she had ever seen in captivity (this coming from a lady who had personally seen and evaluated every captive bear in the country). While I realize that very little of this chapter has actually been about Doug Seus, it all nonetheless shows how he is able to do what he does. By tapping into a part of the bear mind that is mostly hidden and unknown, a secret that the bears themselves are doing a pretty good job of keeping a tight lid on, and by building and sculpting a relationship based on trust and respect, he is able to share a bond with his bears that is not too dissimilar – and perhaps even more rewarding – from the average Joe and his dog.

Chaik (top) and Killisnoo (bottom) being their usual curious selves at Fortress of the Bear. Photos by the author.

Chaik (top) and Killisnoo (bottom). Photos by the author.

35

Now others such as Casey Anderson, owner of the Montana Grizzly Encounter in Bozeman, are following in the footsteps of Doug's incredible work. Casey has successfully raised, tamed, and trained a young, lost grizzly bear named Brutus to be his best friend and companion. They've become so close that Brutus served as best man at Casey's wedding and occasionally even joins the family at the dinner table. Now Casey and Brutus travel the world, exploring its wild places for their television series *Expedition Wild*.

## GRIZZLY ADAMS

Any proper discourse about bear training and trainers would be remiss to exclude the famous Grizzly Adams of the 1800's (not the Dan Haggerty TV character), who was perhaps the first person to have grizzly bears as companions. Although his bears were not obtained as cubs from some form of squalid captivity, and his training methods were not as kind as Seus' and Anderson's, the end result was no less extraordinary.

John Adams (aka James Capen Adams) was born near Boston, Massachusetts in 1812, but ultimately landed in California after being taken West by the Gold Rush. Those were the days before the loss of California's grizzly population, so Adams set himself up as a hunter and trapper.

In 1853, he set out on an expedition to western Montana where he captured a yearling female grizzly that he named Lady Washington. At first, the little cub proved to be a violent and angry force to be reckoned with but, after rewarding her ferocity and ill-temper with his own in the form of brutal beatings, Adams noted that she seemed to learn her place and followed him around like a dog.

Over time, he trained her to carry packs on her back and pull a loaded sled. She even allowed him to ride her like a horse, shared his meals, and accompanied him on hunting expeditions in which she would cuddle with him on cold nights to keep him warm. Adams would later say, after she had stood defensively by his side during an encounter with a wild grizzly, that she was his closest companion and that "I felt for her an affection which I have seldom given any human being."

Perhaps the most extraordinary example of the bond and loyalty they had established between themselves was an incident in which Lady Washington began an affair with a wild grizzly that had been visiting Adams' camp at night. Adams disapproved of the relationship and the Lady seemed to sense that, for she ultimately refused to leave behind her domesticated life in favor of a wild one, though she did later give birth to a cub that Adams named General Fremont in honor of the American military officer.

In 1854, Adams captured a two-week old male grizzly cub from a den near

Yosemite Valley. He named the little bear Ben Franklin and set about on the same taming and training regimen he had perfected with Lady Washington. In 1855, Ben saved Adams's life by viciously attacking and fighting off a mother grizzly after it had aggressively mauled the man. Both Adams and Ben suffered severe wounds in the encounter, including a head wound that would claim Adams' life in 1860. On several other occasions, both Ben and the Lady fought valiantly to protect Adams from fierce grizzlies they encountered on hunting expeditions.

Other bears eventually came into Adams' life, including Samson, a monster weighing in at 1,500 pounds. Adams gave up hunting and began traveling with his animals as a type of living museum. He could often be seen walking the streets of San Francisco with Lady Washington and Ben Franklin following faithfully, and unrestrained, behind. Ben Franklin died of an incurable illness on January 17, 1858 and the San Francisco *Evening Bulletin* ran his obituary under the headline "Death of a Distinguished Native Californian". Adams later relocated his animals to New York City where he established a partnership with P.T. Barnum.

Personally, I find accounts like these to be extraordinary. Considering what these trainers have been able to accomplish, there clearly seems to be something more complex than just base wild animal instinct going on inside the mind of the bear and this is what finally hooked me and is what still fascinates me today.

## VITAL GROUND

So great was Bart the Bear's intelligence and so unfailing his loyalty that Doug and Lynne decided that Bart could be in a unique position to serve as an ambassador for his wild cousins, standing for habitat conservation and teaching the next generation to have respect for all living things. Thus, they formed and launched their non-profit conservation organization Vital Ground in 1990 with the purchase of 240 acres of rich bear habitat adjoining protected land in Montana.

Bears are an umbrella species and their presence, or lack of it, is indication of the overall health, or lack of it, of an ecosystem. Bears will only go where the land is good and if that land is healthy enough to support them, it's healthy enough to support all creatures. "Where the grizzly can walk, the earth is healthy and whole," says Lynne Seus. Vital Ground addresses the issue of habitat loss by working to protect and set aside areas of prime habitat for grizzlies and other wild creatures. Many of these include linkage zones connecting grizzly bear ecosystems and phasing out small islands of genetic isolation. The end goal will be to link grizzly populations in the lower 48 states with the much larger populations of southern Alberta and British Columbia.

To date, Vital Ground has helped protect almost 600,000 acres of crucial wildlife habitat in Montana, Idaho, Wyoming, Alaska, and British Columbia. Bart the Bear may be gone but his legacy lives on as a bright light of hope and promise for all the bears who are struggling to survive in a rapidly deteriorating wilderness.

For anyone who is exposed to Doug's work, either through internet videos, the varied films that feature his bears, or a lucky public appearance, there can be no doubt of the man's gift as a bear whisperer and communicator. Watching him wrestle and play with Little Bart and Honey Bump while they excitedly perform a number of commands, all varying from a "happy bear" dance to head-shaking to somersaulting, one becomes privileged to see a side of the bear that is seldom observed, except in the safest and most nurturing of environments.

And the Seus family clearly ranks as one of the best of those.

Doug Seus and Bart the Bear. Photo by Jon Freeman.

# CHAPTER FIVE:

## TOBY, BALOO, AND LUCKY

With the salmon run occurring unusually late in the summer of 2010, wild bears had been coming down to eat from the plentiful berry patches growing along the fence line at Fortress of the Bear, including a mother with three second-year cubs.

After making short work of the berry crop, these four started coming over the fence every night for a week. There were no attractants left out for them and they never did any serious damage, but they did claim the storage barn as their new den and fashioned a very impressive bed out of hay, straw, and shredded paper. It seemed they were making themselves right at home.

Finally, Phil Mooney, the local Fish and Game biologist, gave us permission to capture the family in our second habitat enclosure so that he could radio-collar the mother and track their movements. Rigging a bait trap of fresh cherries, we lured them into the enclosure and slammed the gate on them. The next day, Phil tranquilized the trio with most of the community on hand as spectators, tagged the cubs, and collared the mother. The plan was to release them that night, but the mother had not fully recovered from the drugs, so we felt it best to keep them another night and closely monitor her progress.

Although she was strangely slow to recover, she finally did pull out of it and we attempted to drive them away the next evening. Two hundred firecrackers were thrown into the enclosure and we banged pots and pans while screaming and shouting. Despite everything we think we know about bears, the noise did *not* frighten them and send them stampeding out the open gate; instead it angered the mother and she aggressively attacked the firecrackers, biting and snapping at them even as they exploded in her face. This should be a cautionary lesson for those who insist on making too much noise while recreating in bear country (see the epilogue for further thoughts).

41

Our tactics exhausted, we went home and the trio finally departed on their own later that night.

The next morning, the signal from the radio collar showed that the family had moved no more than half a mile away and spent the day bedded down on a hillside overlooking the Fortress. That night, they again came over the fence and a clear picture was starting to emerge. According to Phil Mooney, a large male bear had been threatening mothers with cubs* at Herring Cove, two miles from the Fortress, and it seemed this mother was bringing her young into the facility at night for protection. I'm sure that a place reeking of humans and two large male bears was a puzzling concept for the female, but she was smart enough to know that a big male pursuing her would not follow her over that fence (in the wild, a female can and will enter a male bear's territory but another male will not). Deducing that people and bears were obviously getting along well here, she knew that it was a safe place to find refuge. Considering their persistence in spending the nights inside the facility (bears often spend the daylight hours bedded down while people are out and active, so the big male would be less active come morning), despite a lack of food sources, and their refusal to leave, I believe this is the only explanation that satisfies all the questions.

By this time, the salmon run was in full swing and most of the bears were moving off into the deep interior of Baranof Island for pre-hibernation feeding. Even so, the mother did not take her cubs off to the streams. They remained in the area as if they would not or could not leave. Then, unsurprisingly, we arrived at the Fortress one morning to discover that bears had been inside again. A perimeter sweep of the outer fence line revealed a very large and very fresh bear track in the mud, one perhaps made by the big male. Phil Mooney gave us the go-ahead to try trapping and if the culprit turned out to be a different bear, we would radio-collar him as well. We rigged the trap that evening and returned the next morning to find the same three cubs as before, only this time without their mother.

Following the signal from her collar, Phil and a trooper found her dead body a few miles away but were unable to visually determine a cause of death. An autopsy revealed that her intestines were clogged with plastic garbage bags. Upon her death, the cubs, having been taught the Fortress was a safe place, returned on their own. We were granted permission to keep them and they still reside there as Toby, Baloo, and Lucky.

*Large male bears often hunt, kill, and eat young cubs. While a cub can make for a convenient snack, they do this primarily to eliminate future competition for resources or to send the mother back into heat.

Having spent so much time living, growing, and learning in the wild, it took the trio a longer time to adjust to the new environment than it did Chaik and Killisnoo but they nevertheless did not shy away from us or try to hide whenever visitors came to see them. They clearly felt themselves to be in a good place and they never exhibited any desire to get out and go elsewhere.

Now they are at least as fully socialized as are Chaik and Killisnoo. Toby, the female of the three, was from day one so expressive with her paws that she now regularly "prays" in front of visitors when asked to by a keeper. Baloo, so named due to his physical resemblance to Asian bears of which *Jungle Book's* Baloo the Bear was based, has come to enjoy getting his head scratched just like Chaik and enjoys licking the hands and face of anyone brave enough to let him, and Lucky, a name given due to his tagging number of 13 and the badly injured leg he came in with, has traversed the long, hard road from shy reclusiveness to the sociable antics of his siblings.

Now, two years later, I still wonder about the circumstances that brought them there. Why didn't the mother take them away to the salmon streams? If the big male was still after them, why didn't he go to the streams himself? Maybe he did, while still making a point to harass the family whenever possible. Maybe he was long gone and the mother had already been forced to turn to eating garbage as a means of keeping her and her cubs alive and that became an addiction that she couldn't break.

There are no clear answers, but the story does offer insights into just how intelligent some bears really are. This mother knew that a facility carrying the scent of both humans and two big male bears side by side would be safe for her and would repel her pursuer (a fenced-in recycling center was right next door and was not used by the family). Even if she was unable to wrap her mind around the idea of this shared territory, she could reason well enough to use it to her advantage and ultimately saved the lives of her cubs in the long run by teaching them that it's where they should go for safety.

Mothers with cubs have a reputation for being the most dangerous and unpredictable of all bears, particularly when around people, but, as we'll see later, more than a few have been enterprising enough to use the presence of humans as a safety zone to protect their cubs from even greater dangers.

Top: Lucky and Baloo asleep on a fiberglass pipe. What's holding Lucky up there? Bottom: Toby praying. Photos by the author.

# CHAPTER SIX:

## THE WAGES OF FEAR

Canadian naturalist Charlie Russell has done some of the most revolutionary work ever attempted with wild bears.

Charlie Russell is not only the man who helped me finally overcome my fear of bears, but is the man who opened my eyes to new possibilities never before considered, setting me on the path that I now follow, inspiring me to start writing on the subject myself. His book *Grizzly Heart* asked many of the questions I had been asking and offered some of the most sensible and thought-provoking answers I had ever heard. The book stands alone as some of the most important work that has ever been done with wild bears.

The son of well-known naturalist, author, and filmmaker Andy Russell, Charlie grew up in Alberta, where his travels with his father early on shaped his perceptions of these fearsome animals. Traveling across Canada and Alaska to shoot their film *Grizzly Country*, Charlie, his father, and brothers became privy to a side of the great bear that was not readily known. Many of them seemed quite sociable and emotional and none behaved as aggressively as it was believed they would. When Julie Helgeson lost her life at Granite Park Chalet in 1967, Charlie and Andy personally investigated the site and the question lingered in their minds as to what would cause these normally shy animals to sometimes kill.

It wasn't until after many years of ranching in grizzly country that Charlie began to formulate the theory that perhaps bears were intelligent enough to return respect when it was given and to pay back mistreatment with the same. Performing an experiment, each spring Charlie would leave the carcasses of winter-killed livestock at the den site of a grizzly that had chosen to hibernate near his property, hoping this would satiate the bear enough upon awakening to prevent it from killing his cattle. As he recreated the experiment each year, he found that the bear seemed to recognize his respect and returned it by never harming his cattle. The neighbors, however, who did not respond as kindly to the bear's presence, did not fare as well; they lost several of their stock to the animal. Charlie even describes an astonishing incident in which he observed the grizzly strolling casually across his ranch, weaving around and among his strangely unfrightened cattle, never once harming any of them. Did the bear recognize Charlie's actions as friendly and respond in kind? It certainly seemed that way, though Charlie feels this could also have been simple luck on his part.

The possibilities fresh in the back of his mind, Charlie visited British Columbia's Princess Royal Island in the early 1990's with a film crew to make a documentary about the rare spirit bears that inhabit the area. On an island with no human population, the bears seemed curious and friendly and Charlie established a unique bond with the young spirit bear who was the subject of the film, as documented in his equally wonderful book *Spirit Bear*.

A few years later, while working as a bear viewing guide in the Khutzeymateen Valley of British Columbia, Charlie was approached by a young grizzly bear while sitting on a log. The bear allowed him to run his hands over her body and even feel her teeth. She seemed equally as curious about him as she slowly reached out a paw to touch his hand. All of these bears lived in protected areas, sheltered from guns and human violence, with only limited and positive experiences with people. As a result, they had not learned fear of man and did not behave aggressively at the presence of man.

Charlie formulated a theory that bears are not born with an instinctive fear of man, that it must be learned, and that the proliferation of that fear would likely only create a situation in which the bears would be *more* dangerous to man, not *less* so. To test this theory in the field, Charlie and his partner, artist Maureen Enns, settled on an enormous, uninhabited wilderness preserve on the Kamchatka peninsula of Russia, home to one of the world's largest populations of grizzlies. With the long, dark history between man and bear on this side of the world, Charlie felt there was nowhere in North America where this experiment could be safely conducted.

The initial experience in Kamchatka did not go well. First, Charlie was disheartened when the bears behaved as if they *were* afraid and ran away without hesitation, and then was devastated when well-known photographer Michio Hoshino was killed by a grizzly at nearby Kurilskoye Lake. This bear was not only food conditioned but was constantly bullied and harassed by Hoshino's Russian crew, its aggression escalating in return…and perhaps in warning, but it nevertheless sparked heated arguments between Charlie and Maureen, both of them questioning the wisdom of being out there and debating whether or not there was a place on earth truly untouched by man. Then, while out exploring one day, Charlie encountered a mother grizzly with cubs. The mother did not seem at all distressed by his presence and even casually lied down to watch him, head cocked curiously to one side. Realizing that the wind was blowing his scent away from her, Charlie moved away, hoping she would approach the spot where he had been and get his scent. To his delight, she did just that, but when she caught his scent, she froze and a visible shudder ran the full length of her body. She jumped away and bolted as fast as she could in the opposite direction, so desperate to get away that she left her cubs scrambling to keep up. Obviously she had never seen a human before and did not recognize one by sight, but she knew the smell and it terrified her. Somewhere this bear had encountered that scent and learned that it was a terrible thing. But where? And how? Charlie's determination was re-ignited in the face of this question.

The answer came unexpectedly during a nighttime walk when Charlie suddenly found himself very close to a poacher's camp and a large grizzly trapped in a snare. As the angry bear twisted and struggled to escape, the wire cut deeper and deeper into its paw, causing severe pain and stimulating production of bile in the gall bladder. Soon, the bear would be killed, the body discarded, and the gall bladder harvested and sold on the black market for a small fortune. Charlie couldn't risk freeing the bear; it could have easily mistaken him for one of its tormentors and killed him just as surely as it would have the poachers, so he had no choice but to leave it to its fate. Not long thereafter, Charlie captured video footage of a massive poaching operation led by the director of the Kamchatka Sanctuary himself! The tape was turned over to authorities and the director brought to court for smuggling poachers in and out of the preserve. The director claimed that he blacked out during the operation and didn't know what had happened. He later pleaded insanity and got off scot-free.

Knowing now that the fearful reactions of many of the bears was a direct result of negative human influence, Charlie moved to plan B. He rescued three orphaned cubs from a squalid zoo before they could be put down and relocated them to his cabin in the preserve, intending to raise them as wild animals and test whether or not human contact would ultimately make them aggressive to people. Charlie and Maureen didn't think so, but many of those watching from behind the scenes were not so sure. One of these was Vitaly Nikolaenko, a local naturalist who didn't like having an outsider in his territory, especially one performing an experiment that could prove most of the so-called experts wrong in many of their assumptions. Vitaly insisted the cubs would inevitably turn on Charlie, but when the project continued moving forward with great success and the cubs never became dangerous, Vitaly became increasingly frustrated and threatened that he could easily just shoot the cubs and lie to his superiors that they had become aggressive. Fortunately, this proved to be just bluster and perhaps no small amount of jealousy and, though Vitaly failed to find any evidence that the cubs were becoming dangerous, his fuming tirades against Charlie's work were unceasing and quite unfounded when one considers the enormity of Charlie's discoveries.

The three cubs – named Chico, Biscuit, and Rosie – grew to be self-sufficient wild animals (hunting, foraging, and denning on their own despite Charlie feeding them and providing them with shelter) who were there at the beginning of each summer to greet Charlie and Maureen as they returned for another season of work. Chico, in particular, seemed to sense Charlie's interest and made the greatest effort to connect. She and Charlie developed a friendly greeting involving the intertwining of claws and fingers that they used only with each other; Biscuit and Rosie never greeted Charlie in this way. As the years passed and the cubs reached adulthood, they remained affectionate toward their surrogate parents, despite their ever-growing independence.

Charlie and Maureen also befriended a mother bear they named Brandy. They never made any effort to interact with her or catch her attention...until she started using them as babysitters for her cubs. She even allowed Charlie to walk in formation with her and her family. Charlie was most surprised by this and recognized this high degree of trust and acceptance as coming from an intelligent, thinking animal that had the ability (and the willingness) to adapt to this change in her environment.

Each summer for six or seven years, Charlie and Maureen returned to Kamchatka and each time they were warmly greeted by their bears. The relationship between them never changed. Sadly, Rosie eventually fell prey to a large male bear and, with the poaching operations taking a heavy toll on the salmon runs, many of the bears were forced to migrate out of the valley in search of other food sources. Chico went with them and disappeared to parts unknown. In the fall of 2002, Biscuit was pregnant with her first litter of cubs and Charlie and Maureen were looking forward to their return in 2003, this time as grandparents.

Unfortunately, in late 2002/early 2003, the poachers – smarting from the victories Charlie had won against them – invaded the preserve and killed every bear they found, including Biscuit and Brandy. When Charlie returned in June 2003, a single gall bladder was nailed to the wall of his cabin, a clear spite of everything he had been attempting to do. Those people needed the fear of bears to be rampant in order to sustain their way of life and to avoid public opposition to their work and they couldn't allow someone like Charlie to rock the boat. Neither could the bear experts, who refused to let go of the dogma that bear/human interactions will always create a dangerous animal, when in actuality it's more often human ignorance of bear behavior and needs that creates the danger. Case in point, in 2008, the poaching of spawning salmon in Kamchatka reached such devastating levels that it created a nightmare situation straight out of a horror movie. A group of Russian mine workers and geologists found themselves trapped in a platinum mine and surrounded by as many as *thirty* starving bears! If there truly is a monster lurking somewhere out there in the dark, it exists as a product of our fear. That's what always creates the monster, in one form or another. As desperate as these people were to silence Charlie, they only proved him right in the end.

Charlie returned to Kamchatka several more times after the tragedy of 2003, this time without Maureen, and successfully raised and released seven more orphan cubs. He finally left for good in 2007 with no desire to ever go back. Now he's bringing his message home to his native Alberta, hoping to put what he learned in Kamchatka to good use in bear/human conflict zones. In October of 2012, Charlie went on an extensive tour of speaking engagements, attempting to tell his story to anyone who would listen. The presentations "went very well," he told me in personal correspondence. "People do get some of the things I hoped for; not all of them, though."

The fact is that many of Charlie's ideas are pretty revolutionary, especially to a public conditioned to fear bears to an overblown extent. "What we have never learned is to be nonchalant around bears and it is getting to be more unimaginable all the time that we can develop this," Charlie told me. "Bears in general are too much like celebrities to us except we are afraid of them. We cannot just accept them and carry on what we are doing and let them do what they need to do, which might even be sitting on the deck with us, enjoying the same scenery we enjoy."

While the general public may be more receptive to this message than expected, it's the wildlife managers who take the greatest issue with Charlie's message. "Most people in a bear management capacity deliberately dismiss and then confuse what I have done into something inappropriate because it suggests that it is okay to be close to bears. They do this because what I am really suggesting is that they, the managers, might be creating dangerous bears by their very policies of being abusive to bears. Not being an abuser myself, the only way I could study this question was to be kind and see if that was a problem. I found they like people if they are allowed to and I did not beat them away from me. That resulted in us being together and comfortable and safe. Because I found that profound trust was possible with grizzlies and black bears if you did not beat up on them, an important question arises: Why are bears becoming increasingly impatient and violent in our parks? Could it be that they are never rewarded for their efforts to get along with us and they are just getting sick of trying?"

That brings up the issue of fear. Are bears really born with a natural fear of man or is it something they must learn? As intelligent as bears are and with their high capacity for learning, little cubs are blank slates. They must be taught by their mother how to find food, what to eat, what not to eat, how to make a den, etc. What she fears, they fear; what she ignores, they ignore. Personally, I think Charlie is dead on in his assumptions. Fear of gun-toting humans is something that must be learned firsthand. But does controlled hunting and aggressive diversionary techniques create a safer animal to hike and recreate with as most wildlife managers claim or does it increase the danger of an unprovoked attack?

I posed these questions to Stephen Stringham, a biologist well known for his "unconventional" views about bears. Like Charlie, Stringham has also raised orphaned cubs in the wild and has developed keen insights into bear psychology as a result. He says, "Most serious or fatal attacks are defensive, not offensive. So hunting or harassment that heightens fear of people may increase risk of a person being attacked in a close encounter – even if greater fear reduces likelihood of bears encountering people on purpose.

"My firsthand experience is that coastal Alaska brown bears are much more defensively aggressive where they are hunted than where they are protected.

That hunting bears gives them a greater respect for people also contradicts logic. While it makes sense for animals to submit to dominants, so long as submission increases safety, submission to a predator would be suicidal."

I ask him about fear; does it exist from birth or do they learn it as they grow? "Animals are born with a certain set of instinctive defense responses that could be triggered by certain stimuli, such as fire or the presence of a natural predator," he says. "However, there are so many potential dangers and so many variables in responding to those dangers, that a whole system of instinctive fears is unworkable. A better strategy would be what is called xenophobia, an aversion – not exactly fear – of anything unfamiliar. I suspect this is actually the source of what we perceive as natural fear in animals, particularly highly intelligent animals like bears. However, as animals come to know people better and better, their experiences with people govern whether their attitudes specifically towards us are fearful, hateful, respectful, or trusting."

And he should know a thing or two about trust. In summers, when he's not teaching at the University of Alaska in Soldotna, Stringham leads bear viewing expeditions into the heart of Katmai National Park where eager photographers and bear enthusiasts can watch coastal grizzlies up close. These bears are neutrally habituated to people, meaning they do not associate humans with food or with danger, so they are fully trusting of their visitors. Many of these bears pass within feet of awe-struck viewers while barely giving them a disinterested glance and mothers with cubs will often foil predators by bringing her cubs close to these large groups of people, using them as a safety zone.

A similar situation exists at McNeil River Falls, also within Katmai. Thousands of people flock here every year to observe massive bears gorging themselves on the plentiful salmon runs. There has never been an aggressive or threatening conflict in the 30+ years that people and bears have been sharing this space. Then in 2007, Alaska Fish and Game made it legal for trophy hunters to take bears in the off season to ensure they would not lose their "natural fear of man", fear that was obviously apparent in the number of bears who fed, slept, and nursed cubs within touching distance of humans. In response to this decision, the department received over 10,000 outraged letters and petitions from all over the world - many of them declaring the unfairness of hunting bears that have learned to trust people, essentially stabbing them in the back – and they miraculously reversed their decision and banned all hunting in the area.

Meanwhile, bear attacks in Alaska have increased as the hunting has increased. More than half the people attacked by bears in the state since the

1970's have been either hunters or hikers and campers carrying guns. 2,000 miles away in Montana and Wyoming, attacks have decreased by 30 percent after grizzly hunting was fully illegalized in 1991. Wildlife managers disregard these correlations, claiming that they don't prove anything, but personally I see a very clear pattern of cause and effect.

Doug Seus says that his bears are smart enough and impressionable enough to learn new commands in only one repetition and that they can clearly recall past traumas and even carry grudges. When Little Bart was being transported to Utah from Alaska as a cub, he recovered from sedation to find himself restrained by ropes. He flew into a wild panic. During a training exercise several years later, a rope caught around Little Bart's ear. Immediately, he flattened his ears and bellowed in anger until the rope was taken away. "He remembered that trauma," Doug said.

The legend of Old Groaner is one that has been told and re-told in every corner of Alaska. Old Groaner was a large man-eating grizzly with an oddly misshapen jaw that inhabited the upper Unuk River country near Ketchikan in the 1920's and 30's. He received his name from the enraged moans, groans, and bellows that would echo from him whenever he caught the scent of man in the forest, a scent that he pursued with a relentless hatred. When the bear was killed in 1935, it was found that five bullets had been embedded in his skull, the right side of which was completely shot away, for twelve years. The cheek bone was destroyed and the jaw hinge shattered. Two lead slugs from a .33 caliber rifle and three bullets from a .33 caliber revolver were all wedged into the right jaw. Was this bear just an indiscriminate killer or was he made into one through years of human abuses?

"From what I have decided about bears becoming predators," says Charlie Russell "is that it is initially about the disrespect that we create in them that sets the scene for what they might do to us if they run out of food, rather than the loss of a food source itself. If they decide they like you, you are pretty safe no matter what goes on in their year to year lives.

"I personally will always be afraid to be around both grizzly and black bears that have had a lifetime of aversive conditioning or a lifetime of being hunted. They have long and acutely good memories that might eventually be triggered by a surprise encounter into inflicting some of that violence back*, especially a protective female with cubs."

Jill Robinson, founder of Animals Asia, has devoted her life to rescuing bears from the horrors of bile farms in which the bears spend their lives in cages barely bigger than their bodies, with rusty catheters inserted into their

*See the following chapter on Timothy Treadwell.

gall bladders to drain the bile. Living their lives in continuous pain and misery, many of these bears chew off their own paws or bash their brains out against the bars of their cages. Robinson has said that when new bears arrive at the sanctuary from the bile farms, they are initially hostile and aggressive towards their keepers until they learn that these humans are different and are not going to treat them cruelly. When I asked Jill whether or not she believes fear of people causes increased aggression towards people, she forwarded my question to two members of her staff who are more hands-on in dealing with the bears. Their responses follow.

Annemarie Weegenaar, vet and bear team manager of Animals Asia Vietnam: "Most aggression I have seen in our bears I would say is mainly caused by fear. Their fear of humans gradually gets less over time when they realize they get offered good food, water, and toys to interact with and the source of fear has been removed.

"I think the routine we provide to our bears seems to settle them as well. I think a lot of their fear may come from uncertainty, e.g. when do they get darted next. Many of them seem fearful initially of the metal hooks we use to clean the cages and other cleaning tools with long handles like brooms, squeegees, etc. I assume they associate this with a blow dart but, as above, when they become accustomed to the routine they no longer seem to be fearful of these tools. We do have a few individuals who continue to be a bit more fearful compared to others, even after having been on the site for a long time. They seem to have a deep-rooted mistrust and would rather not come too close to us.

"I would agree with the assumption that making animals fearful of people might actually make them more aggressive. But I do think if the bear has space to get away from the source of fear, they would still rather do so than approach aggressively. But I would not put my hand up to try this in practice!"

Nicola Field, vet and bear team manager of Animals Asia China: "I think you have summarized this quite well. I would say it is a fair overall assessment that bear aggression towards people is based on fear and, especially with the bears we rescued, a deep-rooted and learned response. We have seen time and again bears who are newly rescued that have displayed aggressive behavior which, with time, TLC, and a nutritious diet, decreases. I think the key thing is that every bear is individual in their level of fear and aggression, how they respond to fear and their own individual experience with humans and how deep-rooted that fear is.

"I think it is also worth pointing out the forgiving capacity bears have. Even down to our ability to weigh and load bears with positive reinforcement, given their backgrounds, I think is a remarkable testimony to their stoic nature but also shows how accepting they are with reassurance."

So what do bear managers and wildlife officials have to say about all this? Predictably, not much. They either write off Charlie's work, disregarding his findings on the basis that he got too close to bears and may have taught others to do the same, or they attack him for habituating the bears and making it easier for them to be killed. In truth, Charlie's bears were wary around anyone except him and Maureen and some individuals with negative attitudes – such as Vitaly Nikolaenko – they outright disliked. To disregard all those facts and say that habituation alone is what killed those bears is to woefully miss the point: fear and the need to keep that fear alive is what killed Charlie's bears, not peaceful human interaction.

On the subject of wildlife managers and how they're dealing with bear issues, Charlie says, "I don't know what most scientists are doing and I have two bear biologist brothers. After all the studying they do, I do not even recognize the animal that they describe most of the time. And too many conservationists use the grizzly mostly just as a tool to protect or establish wilderness by insisting that to survive the bear needs empty, people-less land (that humans have no use of), ignoring the fact that this is a disservice to the bear because what grizzlies really need is for people to just relax a bit and let them share some good productive land on their ranch or along a road, etc., and even in our parks without their mere presence causing a huge commotion and if they happen to decide to not be afraid of people, that should not automatically lead to their deaths."

But Charlie admits that the fear of bears is so deeply ingrained into us from so many different sources that it is not easy to simply push it aside, even for him. Several times while interacting with Chico in a playful manner, the bear would try to escalate the play and take their interaction to another level, prompting Charlie to quickly push her away, alarmed by the sudden, unexpected behavior. He writes in *Grizzly Heart* that she would respond with a pained look, one that seemed to say "What have I ever done to hurt you?" He knew that she never had and never would but decades of sensationalized media stories and Hollywood monster bears threatened to override what he logically knew to be true and could have damaged the relationship of trust and respect he had established had he allowed it to.

If indeed there is a beast lurking out there in the shadows somewhere, waiting to snag us when we're unprepared or dismember our children while they stand at the bus stop, it's not a grizzly bear; it's fear. Fear of the dark, fear of the unknown, fear that there may be some silent creature stalking through the woods in search of a victim. Fear is the real monster and the most difficult of all to overcome.

Charlie sharing a tender moment with Chico.

# CHAPTER SEVEN:

# THE LEGACY OF TIMOTHY TREADWELL

When you think of Timothy Treadwell, the first thing that comes to mind is probably exactly what the media has told you to think: bear lover killed by the animals he thought were his friends. While that headline certainly makes for good Hollywood fodder, the reality is much more complicated.

Timothy Treadwell was born Timothy Dexter in 1957. An aspiring actor, he changed his name to Treadwell and moved to Hollywood. His acting career never took off - though he was just barely beaten out by Woody Harrelson for the role of Woody Boyd on *Cheers* - and he got involved with the wrong crowd. After a brush with death from a drug overdose, a military buddy of Timothy's encouraged him to find a passion in his life to pull himself out of his self-destructive spiral. Having always wanted to see Alaska, Treadwell struck out for the Last Frontier. Awed by the beauty of the mountains and the vast emptiness of the country, Treadwell had his first bear encounter on that trip. Overwhelmed by fear, Treadwell instinctively began to sing a song, more as an exercise to keep himself calm than to soothe the bear, and the animal turned away and let him be. The encounter ending more peacefully and amicably than Treadwell expected, he, like many others, began to wonder if there was more to bears than met the eye. This became his passion and he wanted to know more.

Returning each summer for several years to the Hallo Bay area of Katmai National Park, Treadwell began trying to forge relationships with the large, salmon-eating coastal bears that inhabited the area. During the winters, he hit the lecture circuit, speaking in schools about bears, how unfairly demonized they are, and how important it is to work for their conservation. Kids loved him and eagerly anticipated his return each winter with new photographs and tales of close encounters.

After years in Hallo Bay, Treadwell moved his camp further south along the Katmai coast to Kaflia Bay. Referring to the bay as "The Grizzly Maze" due to its high concentration of large grasslands marked by hundreds of bear trails, Treadwell recorded almost 100 hours of footage, took thousands of still photographs, and filled notebook after notebook with his observations of bear behavior.

During his last three summers Timothy was accompanied by his girlfriend Amie Huguenard, who admired his passion and dedication for the bears, though she herself was deathly afraid of them. On October 6, 2003, Willy Fulton, Timothy's float plane pilot, arrived at Kaflia to pick them up and return them to Kodiak from where they would continue on to Southern California. In previous years, Treadwell was always by the lakeshore with his packed gear, waiting for pickup. This time he was not.

A search of the area revealed the partially eaten remains of both Timothy and Amie and an aggressive male bear protecting the campsite. The bear and a younger adolescent were both killed and Treadwell's video camera was recovered at the site. Curiously, it had been turned on just prior to the attack that claimed his and Amie's lives, but there was only an audio recording of the incident, no video.

Needless to say, in the wake of their deaths, the media had quite a field day. Headlines such as "Wildlife Author Killed, Eaten by Bears he Loved" swept across the nation until Treadwell essentially became known as the man who committed suicide by bear. Ever since, bear advocates who spend their lives trying to teach people about the peaceful, more docile side of bears have had the stigma of Treadwell hanging over their heads like a dark cloud. Working at Fortress of the Bear, hardly a day went by when we were not asked our opinion of Treadwell.

Mention Timothy's name to almost any wildlife managers or "bear people" and you'll either get a scoff of disdain, a flurry of profanity-laced rants, or an uncomfortable silence from people who wish the whole thing would just fade away. Yes, there is much to say that is critical of Treadwell and his tactics but there are also good things just depending on which story you bought.

The main criticism is that Treadwell took no steps to protect himself, refusing to use pepper spray or electric fencing. He did utilize those items initially, and even used bear spray to defend himself from a highly aggressive adolescent. In his book *Among Grizzlies*, he writes of this encounter, saying that he was initially upset about the discomfort he caused the young male until it shook off the effects of the spray and came back for another try, whereas he had to blast it again, sending it packing permanently. This time, he wrote, he was not sorry about having sprayed the bear; tough aversive conditioning was exactly what an overly bold animal like this needed to survive.

This one incident aside, his efforts to establish a trusting relationship with the bears was for the most part successful. Many bears even slept outside of his tent. While Treadwell was very knowledgeable about bear psychology and body language, this was also one of the most popular bear viewing sites in the world with thousands of people flying in every summer to walk the shores of Hallo Bay with these majestic animals. All of the bears were neutrally habituated to people (meaning that while they were accustomed to the constant presence of people, they didn't associate people with food or danger) and many knew that staying near Treadwell would put them in a safety zone and protect them from larger, more wary bears. Timothy began to feel bad about using pepper spray and electric fences against these animals and stopped carrying even the most basic protection. This raised the ire of many bear viewing guides along the Katmai coast and of other naturalists such as Charlie Russell.

"Timothy has made my life difficult, both while he was alive and after he died," Russell says. "Before he was killed, he tried zealously to undermine my credibility. Some years ago I had offended him by writing in my book *Grizzly Heart* that he did not carry pepper spray nor use electric fencing around his tent to protect himself. I did not say this was wrong, only that I did things differently. There seemed little doubt to me that camping on major bear trails in thick brush was putting him at the mercy of a possible transient bear that he would not have built any kind of trusting relationship with. He angrily told me that he was essentially a trespasser in their territory and therefore he did not want to hurt them in any way. In answer to this, I confronted him with the possibility that his death could undo everything that he and others were trying to do to change people's attitudes towards bears."

This, apparently, is the possibility that Treadwell never considered. He was aware of the likelihood of his own death, sure; he spoke about it on video many times. But he seemed to miss the impact it would have on his message about bears. Saying that they are not the savage man-killers they're made out to be doesn't hold much weight when you end up getting yourself killed by one.

"During the last 20 years, bear viewing has become a bigger part of the Alaskan economy than hunting them," says Charlie Russell. "Hunters understandably feel threatened about this trend because many photographs show bears and people mingling together peacefully. This has made killing grizzly bears for sport look more like murder than an act of bravery. Hunters desperately needed Timothy's blunder to put the danger back into bear encounters."

The apparent glibness for his own safety and for the value of his work aside, what about the video he shot, the photos he took, and the countless notebooks filled with observations and detailed descriptions of thirteen generations of bears? Doesn't that count for something? Again, asking that question to many in the bear field will only inspire a raving, foaming-at-the-mouth response rather than a serious discussion about the topic.

Biologist Stephen Stringham, who is also one of the most active bear viewing guides along the Katmai coast, is one of the few to see some value in what Treadwell was trying to do and who felt that, with some guidance, Timothy's notes and observations could be put to use in valuable bear studies and that his up-close experience with bears could be fashioned into a world-class educational curriculum for students. The two were in the process of hammering out the details when Tim and Amie were killed. Now, Stringham says, "Jewel Palovak (Timothy's longtime friend and co-author of *Among Grizzlies*) has all his notes and videos and cut off all communication with me at the time she started getting (monetary) offers for his footage, despite the fact that I had spent a great deal of time just after his death holding her hand so to speak by phone. I fear that (Treadwell's) legacy will never advance beyond that of kook."

Despite the seeming recklessness of Treadwell's tactics, Stringham and Russell are quick to point out that this "so-called fool" did survive unarmed and unprotected for thirteen summers among one of the densest brown/grizzly populations in the world. That fact tends to go over most people's heads and Stringham, who is conducting extensive first-hand, field-based research on bear body language and communication, says that while Timothy may not have been the bear whisperer he believed himself to be, he was without doubt a communicator. He could read body language signals and mimic the same to make his own intentions clear. His habit of singing to the bears and speaking to them in baby talk was merely a way of imposing a sense of calmness over himself, one that would come through in his body language and be apparent to the bears, thus keeping them calm as well. This wasn't the mental derangement of a kook; it was in actuality very smart thinking.

But Stringham also knows that the study of bear body language is still young – virtually uncharted territory in Treadwell's time – and some signals can have multiple meanings depending on the situation. Is it possible that a misunderstanding of body language signals and a miscommunication of intent led to the deaths of Timothy and Amie?

# BEAR 141

In the rich, summer world of coastal Alaska, those bears lucky enough to stake a claim along the rugged, storm-swept shores are rewarded with a massive buffet of fat and nutrient-rich salmon. Gorging themselves on 20,000 calories per day, these massive animals (referred to as brown bears but, for all intents and purposes, exactly the same as grizzlies) move up into the mountains with the onset of fall to hibernate. With their departure from the coast, the smaller, thinner, hungrier bears move down out of the mountains, hoping to find scraps left abandoned on the shore, always alert and on edge about the possibility of running into one of the larger coastal bears. It was one of these lean and scraggly transients, from a wilder place with no trace of human presence, that killed Tim and Amie.

We don't know much about how their final moments played out except for what's been transcribed from the audio recorded by their video camera. According to the script, Tim and Amie were packing for the next day's departure when the bear entered their camp. Tim went outside to bully it away (his tactic for dealing with potentially troublesome bears and establishing his dominance over them), and the bear blindly attacked him. Amie shouted at him to play dead and when he gave it his best effort, the bear broke off the attack and walked away. Treadwell did not continue to play dead until the bear was out of sight, however, struggling to get up, screaming and shouting in panic, and the bear returned with a more vicious assault. The transcript ends with Treadwell being drug away and Amie's horrified screams growing louder and more frantic until they're suddenly silenced.

If the killer was indeed the thin transient from further inland (one such bear did indeed arrive on the scene just days prior to the attacks and Treadwell admitted on video that the animal's temperament greatly frightened him), then it was likely apprehensive about the possibility of encountering a larger bear and reacted aggressively as a result. The fact that the bear struck and then moved away would seem to suggest that the attack was in self-defense. A close-range encounter with this strange, upright thing behaving in an aggressive, dominant fashion would have sent an already nervous bear into fight-or-flight mode and it chose, haphazardly, to fight. Timothy's struggling, screaming, and calling for help could have triggered a predatory response and brought the animal back with a different agenda. Amie's panicked screams would have turned that drive into a frenzy.

But there is one more highly disturbing possibility.

The bear believed to be the killer was necropsied and a tattoo was found on the inside of its lip: the number 141. Bear 141 was a research bear and had been for 14 years, ever since the Exxon Valdez oil spill. Every summer since 1989, the bear had been chased down by biologists, darted, tranquilized, tagged, analyzed, man-handled and re-released. Could all those years of stressful treatment at the hands of humans have created an animal that was hostile towards humans? We've already seen how impressionable bears are and how well they remember traumatic experiences. Could the unexpected sight of a human - a human behaving as a dominant at that - have triggered an aggressive attack from the bear? The issue of handling by biologists leading to increased aggression has been brought up repeatedly, becoming a hot topic once more in 2010 when a hiker in Yellowstone was killed without provocation from a bear recovering from the effects of a heavy tranquilizer.

This is all new information to some people as most sources will not cite or even consider these possibilities. Nick Jans' excellent book *The Grizzly Maze* is the only resource I've found on Treadwell that seriously considers anything other than the mainstream media's Hollywood scenario. Just because Treadwell was killed by a bear, it doesn't mean he was wrong about them, no more than the fact that people are inherently good can be invalidated by the rare psychopath who kills a score of women or who shoots up an elementary school full of children. Bears are individuals and individual experiences create individual animals. It took thirteen years, but Tim inevitably found that one, rare individual who, very possibly due to human action, had simply gone wrong.

# GRIZZLY MAN

As if the "bear man killed by the animals he loved" mantra was not bad enough, along came Werner Herzog's 2005 documentary *Grizzly Man* and forever solidified the world's view of Timothy Treadwell as an insufferable, bipolar maniac. Ranting and raving in front of his camera, Treadwell spews a profanity-laced spiel of venom at the Park Service, Allah, Buddha, Jesus, and anything else he can think of throughout the film's two-hour runtime, portraying a man who is clearly on the downhill side of a psychotic breakdown. The film immediately came under fire from those who knew Treadwell, all of them claiming that the movie's depiction was inaccurate and disrespectful.

Even critics who flat-out despised Tim and his methods attacked the movie for presenting a very cleverly edited and false portrayal of a man who they say was finding his purpose with grizzlies, not losing his mind among them. Nick Jans, who had spent countless hours researching Treadwell's life and speaking personally with everyone who knew him expresses his shock and surprise at Herzog's interpretation in the intro of *The Grizzly Maze*. Charlie Russell, Stephen Stringham, and many others who knew Timothy also took issue with what Herzog was trying to do with his film. Surely someone like Treadwell, an aspiring actor with a larger than life personality, a video camera, and plenty of time on his hands would stage scenarios or use the camera as a chance to show off, either for his own amusement or to keep his skills in check. Now put those tapes into the hands of a skilled storyteller like Herzog, a man who is obsessed with madness, whose every film is about the slow descent into insanity, and who believes that nature is an abhorrent place filled with monsters and evil, and what do you expect? Contrast *Grizzly Man* with Animal Planet's *Grizzly Man Diaries*, a mini-series presenting Treadwell's footage in the proper context, as he shot it, and the differences are striking.

I don't think there will ever be a day when Timothy Treadwell is not a topic of controversy, bitterness, and hard feelings, especially for those of us who are trying to advocate a new perspective about bears, as he did. As I've already stated, the fact that he was killed by a bear does not mean he was wrong in saying they were not as dangerous as they've been made out to be, particularly when one considers his technique of dominant behavioral signals and the nature of Bear 141, both of which have gone largely unreported. It is imperative that we take a close look at the media and at how they report incidents like this. I've found that with bear attacks there are usually two sides to the story: what happened and what you're *told* about what happened. The media's penchant for highly sensationalized, overly dramatic material has got to come to an end. Instead of reporting strictly about the horrors of bear attacks, let's explore the reasons why they've happened. As we've seen here, there's more to Treadwell's story than meets the eye but unfortunately that doesn't hold a candle in comparison to the tale of the "mentally ill bear lover" who was killed and eaten by his friends. And I don't know that that will ever change. People don't care about facts or investigative journalism; all they want is a good story.

Timothy Treadwell and his pal Timmy the Fox hanging out along the Katmai Coast.

# CHAPTER EIGHT:

## HOPE FOR BLACK BEARS

Dr. Lynn Rogers watches as a black bear searches for insects inside a log. Photo courtesy of Lynn Rogers and bear.org.

There is no doubt the grizzly holds my attention more than any other bear, or any other *creature* for that matter. Not only are they the ultimate symbol of wilderness but they also present a greater challenge to us than other bears. Here is an animal whose volatility has left a big question mark in the wake of almost all attempts to get along with it, a challenging animal that *demands* your respect and makes no promises about ever returning it, a rogue that – in its arrogance and pride – refuses to conform to any whims our society seeks to place upon it. They make us look a little closer and work a little harder. All one has to do is compare the number of grizzlies in the lower 48 states of North America with the number of black bears to see which is the harder of the two to get along with.

Even though this puzzling enigma of an animal has more than earned my awe and respect, it would be remiss of me to not give black bears a fair shake in this text considering that they are the bear most likely to be encountered by readers. Thus, in this chapter we will be profiling those individuals who have made the greatest contributions to our understanding of these generally shy and timid creatures.

## BEARWALKER

Born in Grand Rapids, Michigan in 1939, Lynn Rogers (see photo, previous page) was terrified of black bears. The hunting and sporting magazines he grew up with depicted blood-soaked drawings and illustrations of slobbering bears with glistening hooked claws tearing hunters, campers, and hikers to shreds. When he began hunting at 16, he "believed bears would charge me in instant anger. I wondered if I could kill a bear before it got me. At 18, I saw my first wild black bear. It ran away."

Fear quickly became fascination as more and more bears consistently did the opposite of what hunting magazines and wilderness lore said they would do. "It took many years for me to overcome the brainwashing I grew up with about bears," Rogers explains. "Finally I began to interpret their body language and their vocalizations in terms of *their* fears rather than *my* fears and I found that I could build trusting relationships with these intelligent wild animals."

In 1967, at age 28, "I began studying them. Now, at 68, I reflect on how these (types of) magazines continue to mislead people."

Beginning his studies in Michigan, Rogers started off hazing black bears away from campgrounds and residential areas for the Michigan Department of Natural Resources (DNR). In the fall of 1969, he moved to northeastern Minnesota and began a broad ecological study of black bears as a Ph.D. candidate at the University of Minnesota. By 1975, Rogers' bear study was considered one of the four top studies of large mammals ever conducted, placing him in the ranks of scientists such as Jane Goodall, to whom he would later be compared.

The study became increasingly complex over the course of the next two decades. Rogers formed trusting relationships with wild black bears, including mothers with cubs and spent 24 hour periods walking and resting with these astonishingly gentle animals, extensively detailing their activities, diet, ecology, social organizations, vocalizations, and more, providing much of the currently available information we now have on black bear behavior. Now Rogers works tirelessly to develop new research techniques focusing on how we can better coexist with black bears as their environment continuously shrinks, and to educate the public about the true nature of these animals. To that end, he and his wife Donna founded and established the North American Bear Center (NABC) in Ely, Minnesota featuring educational exhibits of their work.

On the side, Rogers has written over a hundred scientific articles and has served as senior author on more peer-reviewed papers than anyone else in the world. He has created several museum exhibits and has edited dozens of articles, books, and television scripts. In Minnesota, Rogers worked with the legislature and the Department of Natural Resources to improve bear management. As a result of his educational outreach, people are becoming more understanding of black bears and thus more tolerant of their presence. Today, people are allowing these animals to repopulate parts of the country where bears have not lived for over a century.

If the proof is in the pudding, Rogers has proved firsthand his belief that black bears are not as vicious as their entertainment industry counterparts simply through the thousands of hours he has spent walking and interacting with them in the wild. Some of them placidly allow him to apply radio collars and take heart rate and blood pressure readings while even some mothers watch, calm and unconcerned, as he picks up and examines their first year cubs. Unlike many other biologists, Rogers's technique – he does not use tranquilizers or any drugs – is non-invasive and does not stress the bears. Rogers agrees that those things can be harmful for bears and potentially for people in the long run. In all of this time and throughout all of this up-close, hands-on research, Rogers has never been attacked or felt that his life was in danger. True, he has on occasion misinterpreted body language signals and pushed too close only to get blustered back into his proper place, but these incidents hardly posed any type of serious threat to his well-being.

All of this is remarkable, but it wasn't until January of 2010 that Rogers became well known in the public eye. His inserting of a webcam into the den of a female black bear named Lily, and the subsequent birth of a cub live on the internet, swept the world by storm and corrected one long-held misconception about bears: that they give birth in their sleep. Not only was Lily wide awake throughout the entire process, she stayed that way most of the winter, tending to her cub and only sleeping periodically.

Following the "Lily the Black Bear" Facebook page, the internet exploded with people asking questions about bears, others saying that their perception of bears had changed dramatically after watching the mother and cub in their den, and even one bear hunter posted that he would never again shoot another bear after hearing the cub cry like a human baby.

Amassing a Facebook following of well over 100,000 people, Rogers and his team have installed webcams into bear dens each subsequent winter, forever altering the scientific community's perception of how hibernating bears function* and what they actually do to pass all that time.

With the change in public perception about black bears and the thirst for more knowledge that resulted from the initial 2010 webcam, that first cub was unanimously named Hope by the growing legions of Facebook fans. I spent most of that winter watching the den cam myself and witnessed one of the most remarkable things I have ever seen: as Dr. Rogers approached Lily's den to take heart rate measurements, she emerged to meet him, making soft dove-like cooing sounds to the cub, a black bear's way of reassuring that there is no danger. Essentially, she was informing the cub that this man could be trusted.

For more than a year and a half, fans were able to follow Lily and Hope outside of their den through online updates by Dr. Rogers and his assistant Sue Mansfield, television documentaries and news reports and, finally, the online birth of another cub, Faith, in early 2011. Then, tragically, Hope was killed that September by a hunter over a bait pile while eerie comments appeared on Facebook bragging of "Hope jerky" and "Hope cooked in a crock pot". The NABC released a statement that the shooting of Hope was accidental and the comments about her death were not posted by the same man. Lily and Faith remained near the site of her death for three days before moving on. As I write this in early 2013, Lily has just given birth to two more cubs.

For those who loyally watched the webcams and closely followed the adventures of this bear family, the loss of Hope was – and still is – devastating, but Rogers has tried to remain stoic in the face of this tragedy. He knows in his line of work that attachments are inevitable…and so are losses. After all, he's already experienced a number of them.

For years, Rogers has been pleading with the Minnesota DNR to provide special protections for his research bears. Attempts to work with hunters to keep the bears safe have had their successes and their failures. While most

*Bears are not true hibernators. They spend winter in a den due to lack of available foods that time of year. Their bodily functions slow dramatically but they do not enter a comatose state like other animals. In warmer climates, bears may not hibernate at all.

hunters have agreed to cooperate and spare collared bears, a select minority have seemingly declared war against Lynn and his work. Signs posted by Dr. Rogers politely asking hunters to spare radio-collared bears have often been torn down, leaving honest hunters unaware of the request and a number of study bears have been lost as a result, despite the neon-pink ribbons Lynn attaches to the collars to help them stand out.

After the Lily the Black Bear phenomenon took flight, many Facebook fans pushed for Lynn to ask the DNR to illegalize the hunting and killing of radio-collared bears to prevent the same fate from befalling Lily and Hope. Lynn chose not to pursue that option, hoping instead to work with hunters and educate them about the necessity of research bears. Unfortunately, the end result did not go according to plan. In September 2010, a study bear was killed and the bloody radio collar mailed anonymously to the DNR by the hunter. It's an action many feel was done for spite and one that prompted Lynn to finally move to illegalize the hunting and killing of research bears. Sadly, to this day, Minnesota DNR has publicly stated that they will not offer special protections to these animals.

As opposed to this decision as I am, I can't really say I'm surprised by it. The spiteful moves made against bear researchers, particularly from government employed wildlife managers, makes up a very long and ever-growing list. What is it about these animals that provokes such a strong negative backlash from organizations like this? Are these creatures really that terrifying to people who do most of their work with them from behind a desk? Lynn Rogers isn't terrified of them and he spends most of his time in the woods with them. So does Terry Debruyn, a protégé of Rogers who walked and virtually lived with three generations of wild black bears in Michigan and who now leads guided viewing expeditions among the massive brown bears of the Katmai coast. So is the DNR's stance really about the bears or is it about Lynn Rogers himself and the controversy that has been stirred up by some of his research methods?

## FOOD CONDITIONING AND HABITUATION

The biggest criticism that is often leveled at Dr. Rogers is the belief that food conditioning and habituation are a part of his work. Clearly the bears have to be acclimated in order to allow the researchers to get close and walk with them and a handful of nuts dropped on the ground from Lynn's hand keeps the bears occupied while being fitted with radio collars. This has brought about allegations both from the DNR and members of the general public that the bears will "lose their fear of man" and will become a danger to both themselves and other people. While this may seem like a valid concern on the surface, it's clear facts rather than persistent dogmas that show why these methods do not contain enhanced risk to anyone.

In 1985, Stephen Herrero published his well-known book *Bear Attacks: Their Causes and Avoidance.* Re-released in 2002, it is still considered the most definitive work on bear attacks and staying safe in bear country. Professor Emeritus of the University of Calgary, Herrero was inspired, after the 1967 Night of the Grizzlies, to analyze as many bear attack cases as he could get his hands on and determine if there was any one causal factor that all of these incidents shared; a trigger, if you will, for an attack scenario. His conclusion, due to the number of cases involving improperly stored garbage, was that food conditioning – easy access to human food – and by default habituation to human presence were the big stumbling blocks in the man/bear relationship. Interestingly, in 2005 Herrero recanted many of his previous conclusions in a scientific paper citing the many safety benefits of bear habituation to humans and noting that habituated bears are "less likely to attack" than non-habituated bears. (*From the Field: Brown Bear Habituation to People – Safety, Risks, and Benefits*).

To support that claim, we only have to look at actual documented facts. In the Greater Yellowstone area, habituated black and grizzly bears along roadsides interact with thousands of people annually with no recorded human injury. In the national parks, thousands of roadside bear jams (visitors stopping along roads to view and photograph bears) have occurred every year since 1990 with never a single bear-inflicted human injury documented. In over 30 years of up-close viewing and interaction at McNeil River State Game Sanctuary and the coastlines of Katmai National Park, there has never been a human injury due to bear attack (aside from Timothy Treadwell and Amie Huguenard which, as we've already seen, was a very unusual situation).

This word 'habituation" has been thrown about in such a broadly generalized way so as to almost have no clearly defined meaning anymore, especially in some bear books where the word is used much too freely and is often mistakenly lumped into the same category as food conditioning. Habituation is simply adaptation, a process of acclimating to new things and new situations. A bear that has had positive peaceful experiences with people and that does not consider people a potential food source (what is often called neutral habituation) tends to be very passive and tolerant toward people. They do not view us as potential providers of food or as direct threats to their well-being, so they essentially disregard our presence.

During my two-month stay in Glacier National Park in summer 2012, I was living in one of several cabins hidden in the woods along the Flathead River in West Glacier. For two seasons, a 300 pound black bear had been living in town, foraging on berry bushes up and down the main road and in people's backyards. Never once did he raid anyone's garbage or gain access to anything other than natural foods. Never once was he shot at, hazed, or frightened away by anyone. In fact, the residents of West Glacier were – and still are – delighted to have him around. Each morning it was not hard to find excited talk about where the bear had been seen the evening before and what he had been doing and if he failed to appear for a few days, concern for his well-being spread throughout the little community. During those absences, everywhere I went I was asked if I had seen the bear and everyone was expected to give a prompt and full report to everyone else when he finally resurfaced.

I had not realized it at that early stage but the bear had taken up residence in the woods somewhere near the cabins, meaning that his presence was a regular event for those of us living down there. I finally encountered him while walking home from the river at dusk one stormy evening in August with a friend of mine. As we started down the drive to the cabins (a good five minute walk at an average pace), we saw the bear about a hundred yards ahead coming up the drive in our direction. My friend was excited but nervous and asked me what we should do. We backed up across the road, making sure the bear had plenty of room to not feel crowded and waited. Once he reached the road and saw us, he changed direction to his left and moved out of the drive onto the road, giving us the same clear path we had given him.

Some days later, I was walking alone down the drive in early afternoon and had almost reached the cabins when suddenly from what seemed out of nowhere there was a large animal moving through the thick brush off trail, just about to emerge onto the path right in front of me. I calmly and firmly called "Hey, bear!" I couldn't see him in the brush but he instantly stopped moving. "It's just me, bear!" I announced, by now assured that my voice was well known in these parts. The bear made a slight course correction and instead of popping out on the trail, he followed alongside it, staying in the brush, moving behind me and out of the way. I moved on and once enough distance had been established, he crossed the trail behind me, barely giving me a disinterested glance.

Towards the end of summer, the bear appeared at the cabins one evening hobbling on a wounded foot. No one in town knew what had happened; if he had been shot for some reason, no one would admit to it. I suspect he might have been injured by a grizzly while feeding on the South Boundary Trail and came back to the cabin area because he knew it was a safe place. He stayed hunkered down in the woods for days until he healed up enough to move on.

This guy is a perfect example of a neutrally habituated bear and shows how easy it is to get along with such an animal. He was not deliberately fed by people and so showed nothing less than utmost respect for people and their space. He was never made to feel that people were dangerous and thus was not aggressive or standoffish around us. When he had been wounded, he knew the cabins were the safest place for him to take shelter until he healed.

The Park Service, with their piles and piles of dogmatic beliefs and opinions passed down through the years, alone felt there was potential danger and so they attempted to capture the bear with a clever trap filled with raw, bloody meat. Well, the bear, it turned out, wanted nothing to do with such a horrid mess and chose to forage for grass and berries instead. The Park Service did heroically snare a neighborhood dog in their trap, though, so they at least found proof that it worked. With the community outcry that followed, no further attempts were ever made to capture the bear and he remains the pride of West Glacier, Montana.

Lynn Rogers' bears behave in much the same way. He says, "A handful of nuts enables us to adjust a radio collar or change batteries in a GPS unit. It's also a greeting that reinforces our voices as we approach. The bears don't expect more food and go about their lives, ignoring the researcher. If they even look at us, we wonder why. They have more important things to do. We are neither friends nor enemies. We are not significant food-givers nor competitors. We are just there recording data and/or recording video."

But bears are individuals and not all of them will react the same way to the same stimuli. As complex in their thinking and learning abilities as human beings, a bear's personality is shaped by its genetics, its mother's lessons, and its experiences; the sum total of its life will dictate its nature, just as it does with us.

In his book *Beauty Within the Beast,* biologist Stephen Stringham wrote of a female black bear who was being fed by an elderly couple living in a cabin in Alaska. In time she became a bully, demanding more, and then forced her way into the cabin to obtain any treats she could find. Despite her habit of intimidating the couple into letting her do whatever she wanted, she never attacked or injured them, not even when they proceeded to beat her with a frying pan. With that level of aggressive bullying, however, it's possible that she would have become dangerous, but this type of behavior has been infrequently observed among bear feeders. Stringham later raised her cubs in the wild and taught them to survive and forage on their own.

On the opposite end of that spectrum are Jack and Patti Becklund who befriended, and often hand-fed, several wild black bears over the course of six

72

years, as related in their book *Summers With The Bears*. The animals never became dangerous or aggressive, never bullied for food, never harassed other people for food, never damaged the Becklund's home or property, and promptly disappeared whenever strangers dropped by for a visit. In fact, one of the bears – named Little Bit – was strongly protective of the couple, at one point actually defending them from a strange, unknown bear that wandered into their yard with seemingly unfriendly intentions.

Benjamin Kilham raised several sets of orphaned black bear cubs at his home in New Hampshire and successfully released them as fully functional wild animals, aside from one female who seemed to suffer from some sort of separation anxiety over the loss of her mother.

Charlie Vandergaw is notorious for having fed wild black and grizzly bears at his remote cabin deep in the Alaskan wilderness. He did so for 20 years without ever being threatened or the bears posing a threat to someone else.

And then there's my friend Allen Piche.

\*\*\*\*

Allen fed wild black bears at his home in British Columbia for ten years and he too has never had any problems. Each year between 2000 and 2010, a total of 24 bears would frequent his home for companionship and dog food, 2 miles from Christina Lake, an urban populated area. Even though none of the bears had ever caused problems in the community, Allen was nevertheless arrested and tried on grounds of feeding dangerous wildlife because of fear of the *possibility* that something could happen.

Shortly after Allen's arrest and the cessation of his longtime feeding habits, a sudden rash of bear problems broke out at the nearby lake and an astonishing total of 18 persistent black bears were shot and killed in an area that usually only receives half a dozen bear visits per summer. The obvious conclusion put forth by the Ministry of Environment is that Allen's bears had become so dependent on human food that they had "lost their fear of man" and essentially forgotten how to be wild animals. A scarcity of natural foods that year just made the situation even more volatile. Remarkably, shortly after the shootings, Allen was astonished to find all of his bears alive and well and gathered outside his home to greet him. *None* of them had been responsible for the issues at Christina Lake! Speaking with his immediate neighbors, Allen was delighted to find that they had not had any problems with bears and had not even seen any hanging around.

Now convinced that feeding the bears would not do the damage the Ministry had claimed it would, Allen continued to provide food for them –

though much less this time – and noticed that they began to spend more and more time foraging for natural food in the nearby woods. Undercover officers posing as curious photographers caught Allen in the act and he was arrested once again.

Allen had been a friend of mine for some time and we spoke on a few occasions about diversionary (or supplemental) feeding. He was attempting to make a case to the Ministry, showing how that method could be used to get the bears back into the wild. He was particularly inspired by the information I related in chapter two about John and Frank Craighead and how they discovered that the garbage feeding bears of Yellowstone not only did *not* pose a greater threat to people but also still functioned as wild animals when away from the dumps. Allen gathered all of that information together as part of the presentation he planned to make to the Ministry in his defense. Of course, the Park Service didn't listen to the Craighead's (resulting in a near-catastrophe) so I don't know that one would really have expected the Ministry to listen to Allen.

Diversionary feeding is a very new idea, so new that many balk at it because it involves humans feeding bears. The principle is something like this: When problem bears surface – most often due to a dearth of natural foods – feeding stations are placed deep in the woods as a means of drawing them back into the wild and these stations are moved further and further away each day until the bears have been removed to a comfortable distance. The few states that have put diversionary feeding plans into effect as a more peaceful solution than bullets have reported an almost 100% success rate in solving problem bear issues.

When Allen presented this idea to the Ministry, they were livid at the thought of providing bears with food because of the chaos they were sure would occur, despite the fact that all of the data Allen had gathered supported his side of the argument and the Ministry had nothing but old ideologies to support theirs. Still, Allen is not a wildlife biologist and 10 years of hands-on, practical experience is apparently invalidated by that little detail, whereas the Ministry officers hold the degrees and the official titles and all the lack of facts and experience that go with that, so of course they won. Allen was fined $7,000 and ordered to halt all feeding, while the Ministry concentrates its attention on shooting more bears at Christina Lake, convinced that Allen's bears are the ones causing the problems. What's ironic is that, considering the lack of natural foods at the time, Allen's feeding of the bears acted as a sort of diversionary program in itself, keeping these specific animals *out* of trouble and away from Christina Lake, where they still have not set one foot! They did not grow to depend entirely on human food, they merely used it as a necessary supplement whenever natural foods were unavailable. Unlikely that the Ministry will ever pull their heads out of the sand long enough to see this though.

Regarding this incident, Lynn Rogers says, "Education about the true nature of black bears and about what creates bear-human conflict and what can prevent it can save so many bears. The same principles undoubtedly apply to bears around the world. It's hard to get past the untested assumptions that have been the basis for professional bear management for so long. It's hard to get past the exaggerated fear that drives liability concerns and leads to so many bears being killed unnecessarily. It's hard for most people to see black bears for what they are – basically shy animals trying to make a living while staying out of trouble. Not demons. Not the angry beasts of magazine covers and TV programs. Just the bears that we have come to know and understand in our 45 years of research. If bears behaved the way many experts and the media say they do, we could not have done what we have done with them these (past) several decades."

## A FED BEAR IS A DEAD BEAR?

"But feeding bears is wrong," I can hear the voices cry, followed by that annoyingly overused adage, "A fed bear is a dead bear." I admit, at first glance some of this information does seem contradictory. How is it that all of these people got close to bears, fed them, and did not suffer any repercussions for themselves or anyone else while bears that have obtained food from campgrounds, garbage dumps, and roadside handouts have become troublemakers and even injured or killed people?

The difference is that all of the previously mentioned individuals were just that – individuals. The bears make the food association with those specific people and those people only. Feeding in campgrounds or along roadsides is done by a myriad number of individuals, faces and scents that change rapidly from one person to another so the association becomes more generalized. In that situation, everyone is of potential interest. Dump feeders only know the food itself and locate those concentrations of it by scent. They have no particular associations or attachments to anyone, making them potentially more dangerous in the lengths they're willing to go to obtain that food. At Fortress of the Bear, we limited feeding by visitors as much as possible, restricting it to staff only, so the bears would not generalize that association and expect a treat from everyone who walked in the gate.

The expression "a fed bear is a dead bear" was made up by a couple of campground managers who found it the best way to ensure that people kept clean campsites and did not feed the wildlife. Unfortunately, the slogan has become too broadly used and is now the mantra of bear management everywhere. For usage in campgrounds, I think the slogan is more than appropriate and is overall very accurate. In other scenarios, such as those discussed in this chapter, it holds little water and shows the lack of science behind it, particularly in its failure to recognize that food can be just as effective at leading bears out of trouble.

Unfortunately, scientists are guilty of generalizing too. The one bear that behaves outlandishly, the statistical aberration, somehow becomes the model for the entire species. Yes, bears are individuals and yes some are monstrous, but so are some people.; that doesn't mean everyone who walks the street at night is a Jack the Ripper searching for a victim. With bears, on the other hand, that is precisely the reaction they usually get. Bears that exhibit nervous bluster or that calmly ignore people are shot and killed under the rationalization that any bear that has obtained human food has "lost its fear of humans" (however *that's* supposed to work) and is likely to become dangerous. About this, Lynn Rogers says, "All too often there is no solid science when it comes to the bear-human interface. That is one of the most important areas of bear management and one of the least studied areas of bear biology. Many biologists think such studies are unnecessary because they think they already know the answers. And preconceived notions tend to rely on selective memory rather than on a solid data base that can produce truly scientific conclusions. The passion behind preconceived notions is no less adamant than in politics and religion."

Lynn and Sue Mansfield have been studying a Minnesota rural community in which a dozen or so households have been feeding bears for over 40 years. Through the research they learned that, even though habituated, these bears did not harass strangers for food, they ran from unfamiliar hikers, and they did not approach hunters or bait piles, which is the opposite of what we're told habituated, food-conditioned bears will do. In fact, survival rates for these bears during hunting season was found to be much higher than that of non-fed bears.

These bears knew who their benefactors were. They expected food from certain individuals only and did not carry that association to strangers, recreationists, hunters, or bait piles. In those situations, they behaved as normal bears with full stomachs should. It's the other bears, those having to scrounge for what meager amounts of roots and berries are available to them, that don't have a resource in someone's backyard, that may approach that hiker with a candy bar or that tent that smells of tuna fish sandwiches or that tempting bait pile beneath a hunter's tree stand. They're the ones that could cause problems or be killed.

## STATISTICAL ABERRATION:
## THE PREDATORY BLACK BEAR

It's ironic that, while grizzlies are more aggressive and more likely to attack, black bears, while less aggressive and less likely to attack, are more predatory and more likely to deliberately try to eat you. This is, of course, so extremely rare that most people living in black bear country will not even need to worry about it. But are there answers, explanations, reasons why such attacks may occur? A recent study may shed some light on it.

According to the study, headed up by Dr. Stephen Herrero, 63 people were killed in 59 incidents in Canada, Alaska, and the lower 48 states. The researchers determined that the majority (88%) of fatal attacks involved a bear exhibiting predatory behavior and that 92% of the predatory bears were male.

Unlike grizzlies, mother black bears don't attack in defense of cubs. With claws as slender and sharp as a cats, they can send their cubs up a tree when danger approaches and then scurry up one themselves. Grizzlies don't have that luxury and have to fight rather than retreat. It's lone male black bears that – according to the study – have no familiarity with humans, who pose the greatest threat, suggesting that perhaps males have evolved different behavior patterns than females.

Also unlike grizzlies, these same rogue males are likely to attack more than once. Disturbing tales are told throughout British Columbia of the rampaging black bear that mauled four people and killed two in one vicious attack at Liard Hot Springs* or the bear that killed and cached, one at a time, the bodies of three teenagers fishing in Canada's Algonquin Park. While evidence seems to show that grizzlies exhibit less aggression when unfamiliar with people (unless they have not been exposed to violence), at least some black bears may be the opposite, seeing potential pray.

Some even theorize that in remote parts of British Columbia black bears and grizzlies may have actually interbred, creating a more aggressive genetic strain, despite the two species being notorious enemies. While that is certainly possible, it can't be proven.

---

*This emaciated animal was believed to be a regular feeder at the nearby garbage dump. Rather than being slowly phased out, the dump was abruptly closed and the bear was starving from the lack of that food source. Tragically, due to the aberrant behavior of *one* animal, fifty bears were killed in the area to alleviate public fears.

Dr. Rogers is not comfortable with the subject of predatory black bears. He's a scientist and likes answers, not more questions. He is quick to point out that such attacks are rare and that, in the 45 years he's been working with black bears, he has never encountered such an animal. Only one in a million black bears ever kills a human being, whereas one in 18,000 people will commit murder. "I don't know if you would call a bear like that a demented bear, like some people," he says, "or a super bear that decides 'Hey, I can take a person'."

Fortunately, most people living in black bear country will never run the risk of encountering such a formidable beast. Throughout the majority of their range, black bears are mostly gentle, shy animals. In a well-known historical account from 1873, as re-told in Benjamin Kilham's *Among the Bears*, a three-year-old girl went missing in the woods near Warren, New Jersey. Day and night, neighbors searched frantically for the lost child. When finally found, she was sleeping under a pine tree with bear tracks all around her. She said a big black dog had found her and slept with her every night to keep her warm.

Allen Piche and his bears, courtesy of Allen Piche and thebeardude.net

# CHAPTER NINE:

## SEEK, THE BLACK BEAR CUB

In May 2010, a family in Southeastern Alaska's Excursion Inlet rescued a starving five-pound black bear cub from a flooding tidal flat and took him into their home. Apparently abandoned for unknown reasons shortly after leaving the den – or even emerging on his own if his mother had not survived the winter – he was ten pounds underweight and only a third of the size he should have been at five months of age. The family notified Fish and Game who, initially believing the cub to be a brown bear, contacted us at Fortress of the Bear. I had only been working there for two or three days and was excited about the prospect of interacting with a young cub.

When he arrived the next day, he was already pretty far gone. We immediately started him on a diet of crushed apple slices and a mixture of infant formula and goat's milk. He spent most of that first day curled up in Les' vest while he gave tour presentations to visitors.

We had barely gotten him halfway through that first day when we received a call from Fish and Game. They had positively identified the cub as a black bear (which we could've told them just by looking at him) and, feeling that a black bear would not be a viable zoo animal due to the preponderance of the species across the country, informed us that they were going to take him back and euthanize him.

Upset and angry, we turned to anyone we could for help: the local radio and television stations, community donors, and Fish and Game biologist Phil Mooney – the only person in that department who seemed truly on our side – just to get some voices behind us. We told all of the visitors and cruise ship guests who came out that day what was going to happen and word began to spread throughout Sitka. A "Save the Cub" petition was started onboard that day's cruise ship and Fish and Game began to receive a good deal of negative feedback from the community. Finally, one of the local radio personalities contacted us and told us he knew Jeff Corwin's people and that he would try to contact him in India, where Corwin was shooting an episode of his Animal Planet series. A couple of hours later, Corwin personally called us and told us that if the cub were destroyed, they would broadcast the story to the entire world and put Fish and Game in their place.

At 4:00 that afternoon, the showdown began. Two Fish and Game interns arrived to take the cub. We met them at the gate, refused to let them in, and told them there was no way they were taking the cub. Not wanting a confrontation and already hit with a serious public outcry, they backed down and left. Sometime later, Holly, one of those two interns, personally thanked us for turning them away; she felt the decision was wrong and did not want to cooperate with it.

Fortunately for us, Fish and Game sent two first-year kids to collect the cub against their will rather than actual departmental officials. Who knows how things would have played out in that scenario? Either way, we had discussed the potential risks and unanimously agreed that we had a responsibility and could not let the cub die, especially after he had been placed in our hands for a day. Of course, the newspaper spin was more than a little disheartening. Reporters got both sides of the story and decided to go with the one that made us look paranoid. The department claimed they were merely taking the cub in order to identify the species (which they had already done) and that we overreacted, believing the cub was going to be killed (which they had told us in plain English is exactly what would happen). Tom Schumacher, head of the ADF&G permit department in Juneau, is quoted in black and white print as saying, "Next time we fully expect they will comply with our wishes."

As brutal as this confrontation was, it did pave the way for at least a temporary alliance between the Fortress and ADF&G. A new director was appointed later that summer and the first thing he wanted to do was visit the facility and see the bears. He was appalled by the battle over the cub and even more appalled by Schumacher's involvement in the final decision to kill him. Being head of the permit department, Schumacher should have no say in such matters. The new director personally brought Schumacher to the Fortress to let him see it for himself and he seemed genuinely impressed and surprised. He had never been there before and had no idea what the facility was even like. A new agreement of mutual cooperation was established that day.

The summer of 2011 saw a new director appointed and what essentially seemed to be the dissolving of that agreement. In May, three cubs were found on the shores of Bristol Bay on the western coast of the Alaskan Peninsula. As per the new agreement, Fish and Game notified Fortress of the Bear of the cubs and, because Fortress did not have room for them or the funds to construct new holding areas, the department gave them a short window of time in which to find a permanent home. It was tight but a placement was made with Mike McIntosh and his Bear With Us Sanctuary in Ontario, Canada. Unfortunately, Fish and Game requires that potential homes meet an extensive number of specific, and often ludicrous, requirements and upgrades before cubs will be transferred. That, coupled with the tremendous amount of paperwork and the ridiculously short amount of time allotted to complete these tasks, prevented Mike from completing the upgrades in time and the cubs were destroyed. Mike's criticism of the department for giving the cubs no option other than death was heated and angry.

Ever since Les had started working to make the Fortress a reality, he has been inundated with similar outrageous requests. During an initial inspection of the habitat enclosures, the department took issue with steel bolts jutting one inch out of the walls in a circle around the interior of the clarifier tanks, fourteen feet above the ground. They insisted that the bolts be removed, otherwise the bears would crazily throw themselves against the wall and be impaled. On another occasion, an actual biologist for ADF&G insisted the pool areas be drained because bears don't like water and would not go in it. Well, I can personally attest to the fact that not only do the bears love the water, they spend eight hours a day in the water!

Even worse, in 2009 a tiny, starving cub actually turned up right outside the main gates of the Fortress. The plan was to take the cub in but when Fish and Game were notified, they promptly showed up and shot the cub. The question of why is one that is still asked and I wish there were some sensible way to answer it. As it stands, it seems they merely find bullets to be the easiest response, ruling out the hassle of tracking and capturing the animal, the resulting pile of paperwork, and the tedious task of finding a home, a task made all the more tedious by the department's refusal to put the word out whenever new cubs are acquired. Instead, they wait for zoos and sanctuaries to contact *them* and ask if orphans are available. Not a very wise move and not a move that a supposedly conservation-minded organization should approve of, especially considering how important bears are to the health of an ecosystem, but again it is the easiest route requiring the least amount of effort.

As for the little black bear cub, we successfully nursed him back to health, fully socialized him to people, and named him Seek (the native Tlingit word for "black bear"). He remained with us for almost a month before being shipped off to the International Exotic Animal Sanctuary in Boyd, Texas. Just as lively and playful as ever, he resides there to this day as Scooter.

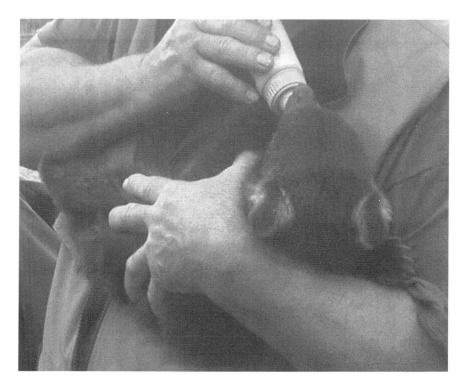

Les Kinnear bottle-feeding Seek.

Me spending the day with Seek.

Top: Seek playing in my lap. Bottom: Seek today at the International Exotic Animal Sanctuary. Photo courtesy of the IEAS.

# CHAPTER TEN:

## LEARNING TO TALK BEAR

Interacting with Chaik.

It was a rare sunny and warm day in Sitka in August 2010; a reprieve from the abnormally cold and wet summer and a calm before the fierce fall storms from the Gulf of Alaska would blow in to hammer the coastline. At Fortress of the Bear, one of our goats from the children's petting zoo had been escaping under the fence. At any weak point he could find, he would use his horns to push the mesh up from the ground and then crawl underneath. I was taking advantage of the slow afternoon and the dry weather to locate these weak points and secure them with heavy metal grates when I heard Les' voice grumbling in a rare note of frustration:

"Killisnoo, knock it off!"

Les is normally a calm man, seldom given to casual frustration so, after tying on the last grate, I decided to go investigate.

"Killisnoo, damn it!" Les' irritated voice echoed to me from the training room area.

Tucked neatly out of sight on the back side of the largest clarifier tank enclosure, the training room/den area for Chaik and Killisnoo is a small dark room with a concrete floor and large steel bars. Between the entrance to the den and the outside habitat is a heavy sliding steel door. When cleaning in the training room, we can slide the door shut and lock it to keep the bears outside or, when going into the enclosure to clean up or hide treats, we can lock the bears inside for the process. Chaik never minded this slight inconvenience, especially when learning that a pile of dog food would be waiting for him in the den, but Killisnoo – his often hyperactive behavior earning him the nickname "ADHD Bear" among the Fortress staff – was getting increasingly impatient with such isolation, even though time spent doing cleanup was minimal.

On this particular day, Les was trying to lock the bears down so he could do this routine work in the habitat. While Chaik placidly munched his dog food, Killisnoo determinedly blocked the door so Les couldn't close it. Each time his interest wondered to the tasty treats, it would be brought right back to Les when he tried to slide the door shut. Chaik raised his head once and watched in what seemed dumbfounded disbelief as Killisnoo ran back to the door yet again and put his front paws up to hold it open.

Les was ready to give up on getting any work done, so I volunteered to try to keep Killisnoo distracted. I opened the cabinet of bear treats and grabbed a condiment bottle of syrup. I sat down outside the bars and called to Killisnoo, holding the familiar bottle up for him to see. He shuffled over to investigate, licked a few drops of syrup off the tip of the bottle, then promptly sat down and puckered his lips in an imitation of sucking on a straw. I held the bottle upside down and he took the tip between his lips, happily sucking on the sweet treat as I squeezed it into his mouth. His eyes drooped half-closed in ecstasy. I very slightly raised my left arm, hidden from the bear's sight behind a cement wall, and pointed to Les. Instantly, Killisnoo bolted back to the door and blocked it again! Needless to say, we got no cleanup done that afternoon.

I've thought about that day often. It's a good example of how bears can read intention through even the most subtle of body language signals. My arm was out of his field of vision but he obviously detected some degree of muscle movement (or perhaps even something in my eyes that gave me away), because he immediately realized what was happening.

In chapter four I talked about how nervous I was when I initially started working with Chaik and Killisnoo. The first time I saw them up close at eye level in the training room was one of the most numbing experiences of my life. Watching Chaik lumbering up to me literally knocked the air out of my lungs and I instinctively took one step back as he approached. He stopped dead in his tracks and just stood there watching me, then turned around and walked back out into the habitat. While that one step back was completely unconscious for me, it spoke volumes to him. He could clearly see that I was nervous and that he was the reason why, so he took himself out of the equation.

For a time thereafter, Chaik was unresponsive and I would say somewhat indifferent to me, like he felt it appropriate to keep a distance. Then, one day, I happened to find him sitting in the training room watching me feed the petting zoo animals. Slicing an apple and sharing it with him, I started talking softly. I told him that I wanted to know how his brain worked, what he felt inside, and what he thought when he looked at me. He stopped eating and focused his attention on me as I spoke. Of course, he didn't understand my words but something in my tone of voice and how that translated into my body language communicated my interest in him and in response he extended one paw through the opening in the barrier and allowed me to touch him. Running my palm underneath his paw pad, he spread his claws and interlocked them with my fingers. He watched this with pointed interest, as if he were just as curious about me. When he tired of the contact, he pulled his paw back and walked away, but he was never again hesitant to approach me. In fact, he seemed to develop a particular affection for me, always wanting to "hold hands" or lick my face. On one occasion, while I spent the afternoon giving presentations to visitors, he sat in the habitat below and watched me throughout, mouth hanging open like a big dog. I've heard many say that bears can sense when someone is interested in them and that they often respond in kind (think cats with cat people). In Chaik's case, that certainly seemed to be true.

The study of ursine body language is a fairly new science and I only know of one man who has devoted his life to developing a full understanding of it. That man is biologist Stephen Stringham.

Dr. Stringham began studying bears in 1969 while earning his BSc degree from Humboldt State University in Northern California. He has since studied black and grizzly/brown bears and other wildlife, including moose, in Alaska,

Montana, New York, Vermont, and Austria. His research on bear communication and aggression began during the summer of 1972 with the neutrally habituated bears of Katmai National Park. Now, 40 years later, he leads guided viewing expeditions in Katmai and has had more than 10,000 close encounters with wild bears. Each of these encounters has been a new lesson in an ever-expanding classroom. He has closely analyzed each encounter and is now putting his extensive knowledge of bear body language and communication on paper. Beginning with *Alaska Magnum Bear Safety Manual* and *When Bears Whisper, Do You Listen?* and continuing in upcoming titles *The Language of Bears*, *Bear Aggression*, and *Grizzlies Among Glaciers*, this series may be among the most important books ever written about bears.

I regret that I can't go as fully into detail as I'd like on this topic, but it would require a large number of figures and illustrations that I don't have on hand and full access to all of Dr. Stringham's assessments, the majority of which are not yet publicly available in print. I do consider this matter to be very critical for proper bear safety, so I do highly recommend reading and studying Dr. Stringham's books as they are released. They can be purchased through the website of the Bear Viewing Association (bear-viewing-in-alaska.info). In the meantime, we're going to look at some of the more basic examples of body language communication in this chapter.

When encountering a bear in the wild, he will react to you the same way he would react to another bear and will send you the same body language signals that another bear would receive. He might be nervous and that could lead to blustery or appeasement behavior. He might be relaxed or curious or could even outright ignore you. Aggression could manifest itself as defensive, offensive, or reluctant. And, very rarely, predation could even be involved. Stringham's work is geared toward identifying these mood signals and knowing what to do to communicate your own intentions back to the bear.

Most bears that you are likely to encounter in the woods are going to be nervous. They honestly have no more an idea of what you're capable of than you do of them, so your presence will likely be a source of great agitation for them. A nervous bear is often very blustery. This is not aggression nor is it a precursor to an attack, but is instead designed to communicate the bear's distress or be intimidating enough to back you off until the bear feels he has enough space to make a run for it. This nervousness can be manifested in several different ways:

- Huffing/blowing: This is an indication that you are likely crowding too close and the bear feels its space has been violated to a potentially dangerous extent.

- Jaw popping: An extension of huffing/blowing. As above, this is nervous bluster, not a threat display.

- Extended lips: Sticking out the lips is often a sign of great displeasure.

- Rapid, flicking gaze: The bear is reluctant to make eye contact (which is often considered a challenge in bear etiquette) and rapidly flicks its gaze from you to something else, then back to you.

- Bluff charges: A bluff charge is much more common than an aggressive charge and is absolutely *not* an attack. It's an attempt by the bear to either put you in your place or push you away so he feels he has enough room to make a dignified retreat. Stand your ground! Bluff charges usually end within only a few feet of the person being charged and sometimes involve ground swatting. Do not run, fight back, play dead, or do anything to escalate nervous bluster into a dangerous situation. Once you've given the bear enough room or he feels he has satisfactorily made his point, the behavior will cease.

Nervousness can sometimes be followed by appeasement. This is when the bear defers to you as the bigger badass and tries to communicate peaceful intent in order to get out of the situation unscathed. Appeasement could manifest in several ways:

- Lowering of head or turning head to side: This communicates submission and unwillingness to engage in anything "messy".

- Backing away: This is deference to you as the bigger bear. Some may turn their back to you. *Do not do the same,* as this could be construed as disrespect and provoke an attack.

- Zero eye contact: Again, a direct intent to avoid a challenge and a subsequent confrontation.

If you're familiar with any type of bear safety information, you'll recognize the above as three of the top safety protocols for handling close encounters. Mimicking these appeasement techniques will communicate your own peaceful intentions to a nervous or aggressive bear.*

In places where bears are used to people and are neutrally habituated, many of them tend to be very nonchalant about encountering hikers and behave in a very relaxed manner.

While hiking with my friend Dave in the Many Glacier area of Glacier National Park in September 2012, we met a young subadult grizzly on the Iceberg Lake Trail. We had been watching the same bear through binoculars as he foraged on the hillside at sunrise and so instantly recognized him when we rounded a bend a few hours later and saw him just up ahead.

He was about a hundred yards or so away and stood in the trail looking at us with his mouth hanging open like a dog (only more regal and less goofy). He had been grazing on wild flowers along the trail and was headed in our direction when we appeared around the corner. He stood perfectly still and watched us to see what we were going to do first.

Dave was nervous and backed away. He quickly reached for his bear spray while I reached for my camera. I instructed him to stand his ground, remain calm, and let the bear take the lead. Having read Dr. Stringham's work, I recognized the open mouth as a body language sign of relaxation. When a bear is completely and totally relaxed, the mouth muscles go limp and the lower jaw hangs open. A closed mouth is not, in itself, a sign of stress, just an indicator that the bear is not fully at ease.

As we watched the grizzly, he turned and moved up the trail in the opposite direction, foraging as he went. More and more hikers piled up behind us to watch the show. As a large group, we very easily could have advanced on him and pushed him away, but being a tough time of year for such an animal, we felt that if he had found a food source, he should be left to it.

We slowly followed the bear down the trail, always maintaining that important 100 yard distance, until he finally moved off the trail into a large patch of sedge grass and allowed us to pass only 20 or 30 feet away from him. I had spent my whole time in the park wanting badly to see a grizzly and I was ecstatic to have gotten my wish that day.

In some cases, bears may directly and pointedly ignore you. If one employs this tactic, he will often look at you long enough to establish that he's seen you then look away and turn his back. If you remain where you are, he may look at you again and then turn away again. This is their way of saying, "I see

---

*A more in-depth discussion about bear safety advice can be found in the epilogue.

you but I'm going to ignore you, so get on out of here!" If this happens, you should move on down the trail and clear the bear's territory. If you continue to ignore these attempts to let you slip by without incident, you could be more forcefully driven away. A curious bear will likely regard you with fully erect ears or may stand up on hind legs. This is not, despite the claims of some sensationalized books, a precursor to an attack. A bear standing on its hind legs is merely trying to see something from a better perspective or catch an elusive scent on the breeze.

Aggression can manifest in two primary ways: defensive and offensive. Reluctant aggression is often displayed during defensive behavior in which the bear recognizes you as a threat to cubs, territory, a nearby carcass, or to the bear itself and the animal reacts to remove that threat.

- Mouth open: This is essentially a sparring pose and communicates to the opponent a willingness to fight if such a course of action is needed. This behavior can also be observed in cases of offensive aggression but with a different set of accompanying mannerisms.

- Ears flat: The ears flattened against the skull signals aggressive intent and is also used to protect the sensitive ears from injury in the event of a confrontation. Also observed in offensive aggression.

- Moaning: Produced mostly as mild warnings to potential threats or out of fear.

- Roaring: Used to either proclaim territory or intimidate an adversary. Anger increasing.

- Raised hackles: The hair on the back of the bear's neck stands straight up, displaying a menacing appearance.

- Turning sideways: An act of intimidation, showing off the animal's size.

- Head down: This signals a reluctance to fight. The lower the head, the greater the reluctance. A moaning/roaring bear with its head down is essentially saying, "I'll fight if I have to, but I would rather end this peacefully."

- Eye contact: While defensive aggression may involve
  some degree of eye contact, a lack of it is an indicator
  of reluctance.

On the opposite spectrum is offensive aggression. Offensive aggression is an angry, violent attack that is unprovoked. In other words, the bear starts it for no good reason. As you'll see, offensive aggression manifests itself in a way somewhat similar to defensive aggression but with a slightly different combination of mannerisms:

- Mouth open: As with defensive aggression, this
  communicates a willingness – or, in the case of
  offensive aggression, a desire – to fight.

- Ears flat: As with defensive behavior, this signals
  aggressive intent and protects the ears from injury.

- Head held high: In defensive aggression, the head is
  held low to signal reluctance to fight. In offensive
  aggression, the head is held high to show willingness,
  if not eagerness, to fight. This is one of the strongest
  possible displays of aggression and makes this set of
  behaviors stand out from a defensive stance.

- Eye contact: Direct, locked eye contact is a strong
  challenge and a sign of high aggression. This is why
  you're told to never make eye contact with a grizzly
  during a wilderness encounter.

On extremely rare occasions, a predatory bear surfaces and while it may certainly be worth your life to interpret these signals, they can be very hard to read and can easily be confused with many of the moods we've already covered. The intent of such an animal often does not become clear until it's ready to make its move.

A predator bear often expresses heavy interest in its prey and may observe you with ears fully erect and eyes locked on target (understand that this can just as easily be harmless curiosity). Most documented accounts of attempted predation have consisted of a tight, dogged approach followed, within the final ten to twenty feet, by the sudden lowering of the head into a stare-down and flattening of the ears. While those last two displays are commonly seen in defensive and offensive aggression, the "locked-on" style of the approach is what gives the animal away. But beware again…even this too can be misinterpreted. Hikers in Montana and Alaska have often reported being followed for miles down trails by persistent bears, only for the animals to continue on their way when the recreationists leave the trail to escape. Bears use trails too and sometimes we just hold them up while they're going about their business.

As you can see, we've come a long way in our understanding of bear body language but still have a long way yet to go. Dr. Stringham is working on understanding how basic human diplomacy can remove the danger from bear encounters and Katmai is one of the best places in the world to explore that dichotomy. Here we have a place where bears not only trust people but respect them as well. "Trust minimizes defensive aggression," Stringham says "And respect minimizes offensive aggression." If a bear respects your place and your right to share the wilderness with him but does not view you as a competitor, he has no reason to behave offensively toward you. Likewise, a bear that trusts you and does not see you as a threat to cubs or a food source has no reason to behave defensively when you're around. They're smart enough to know this and as long as certain boundaries are respected and everyone is speaking clearly, the respect you give will be returned to you.

The more knowledge you gain about bears and the more you learn about their behaviors and habits, the easier it will be read and interpret the signals they're sending you. Working with Chaik and Killisnoo, I learned that it's very much instinctive and that we all possess that instinct, even if we have become somewhat out of touch with it. Have you ever been able to read a person's intentions just by looking at them or had an anti-social cat jump up into your lap if you're a cat person? If so, then you've already experienced it to some degree. Educate yourself as thoroughly as possible about bears and you'll find that learning their language is really not as complicated as it sounds.

Stephen Stringham on the Katmai coast. Courtesy of Dr. Stringham and the Bear Viewing Association.

# CHAPTER ELEVEN:

# BEAR INTELLIGENCE

Because of a bear's slow, plodding nature, they're not generally thought of as one of the most intelligent animals or they are considered to be "uninteresting", much like oversized cattle when, in reality, a bear's brain – particularly that of a grizzly or a polar bear – is almost as complex as that of a human being and they may in fact be the most interesting animal on the North American continent. There is a reason why circus bears are trained to ride bikes and roller skates, play musical instruments, and other routines of such remarkable complexity that few other animals could master them.

What's most interesting to me is that this level of cognitive ability is not often observed among bears in the wild. A possible explanation for this is that a bear in the wild is so driven by the single-minded purpose of survival and storing up enough fat for hibernation that the full scope of what they're capable of must often take a backseat to wild instinct. In a captive environment, however, a bear's mindset tends to be somewhat different.

Doug Seus has said that the original Bart the Bear was at least as intelligent as a chimpanzee and was still not that remarkably intelligent as far as grizzlies go. He recounts a story in which a flash flood had washed a Coke can and a thorny hawthorn tree into a ditch alongside his Utah home. Bart attempted to retrieve the can but was deterred by the sharp thorns. Looking back and forth from the can to a two by twelve plank lying nearby, Bart picked the plank up in his mouth and used it to press the branches down so he could retrieve the can.

Else Poulsen witnessed some of the most amazing evidence of intelligence while working as a bear rehabilitator for the Calgary Zoo. Several of Poulsen's co-workers had told her of the remarkable things they saw while working with the bears but none spoke of it openly due to criticisms of anthropomorphism and fear of losing their jobs. Finally, Else could keep silent no longer and wrote of the incredible things she experienced in her 2009 book *Smiling Bears*.

In it, she describes how one of her grizzlies would ask for a bath by rubbing her paws over herself in a washing motion. During the bath, she would use her nose to point to specific parts of her body she wanted cleaned. If experiencing pain, many of the bears Else worked with would first point with their noses to whatever it was that hurt and then bite down on their paws to indicate pain. One young bear, shunned from play by two older bears, approached Else forlornly, made eye contact with her, and bit down on his paw. Else says, "The message (communicated by the bear) was clear: this hurts."

Poulsen tells the story of a bear who playfully snatched a glove off her hand and thrashed it around in a victory dance. Else quickly stuffed her hand in her pocket to protect it from the bitter cold of the Calgary winter and when the bear did not see her hand, it dropped the glove and stared wide-eyed at the spot where her hand had been. Realizing the bear thought it had taken her hand off, Else pulled it out again where it could be seen. The bear took a good look at her hand as reassurance that it was still attached and merrily returned to thrashing the glove.*

The polar bears Poulsen worked with showed the highest intelligence. One bear, after being given frozen chicken to play with, expressed its displeasure by sticking out its lip then it took the chicken to its pool and threw it in the water. Staring directly at Else to ensure it had her attention, the bear bounced the chicken up and down in the water until it thawed and slapped it into a million pieces, demonstrating its ineffectiveness as a toy.

Lily the Black Bear seemed smart enough to associate her den cam with Lynn Rogers. Whacking it with her paw while playing with Hope in her den, she gazed wide-eyed at the camera, sniffed it, licked it, and cooed reassuringly at it in the same way she would to calm her cub, apparently in an apologetic gesture.

As dark and grim as the story is, Larry Kaniut's *Alaska Bear Tales* tells of a hunter who happened upon two grizzlies. He shot and killed one and pursued when the other, a female, ran. He cornered the bear in a river and she tried to climb the steep embankment to get away, but the slope was too muddy and she slid back into the water. Trapped between the slope and man, the hunter

---

*A similar incident occurred at Fortress of the Bear. When volunteer Debi Terry accidentally dropped one of her gloves into the training room, Baloo promptly picked it up in his mouth and handed it back to her.

said the bear moaned and wailed when he raised the gun and took aim. Amazed, he lowered the gun…then raised it again, getting the same response. Finally, the bear ducked her head into the water and drowned herself rather than suffer the same fate as her comrade.

In Stephen Herrero's *Bear Attacks: Their Causes and Avoidance,* the story is told of a radio-collared black bear being tracked on foot by a researcher while the man's father patrolled overhead in an airplane. In order to throw off his tracker, the bear built several day beds in different locations, entered a stream, backtracked 50 yards, and slipped into thick foliage. The man refused to give up and by late afternoon the sun was melting the snow, exposing the rocks underneath. The bear used this to his advantage, stepping from rock to rock, leaving no trail behind. Finally the researcher picked up the animal's tracks again and followed them until they stopped, disappearing into thin air. This time the bear had walked backwards, placing his feet precisely into his own tracks, and went back in the opposite direction, eluding the man.

In *Among the Bears,* Ben Kilham learned that not only are bear cubs impressionable in their youth and that one traumatic experience during that formative time can scar them for life, but also that they're capable of altruism, a quality that was previously thought to only be found in human beings. But not only did they show altruism for each other, but for other forms of life they encountered!

Testing their intelligence, Kilham presented them with a mirror, hoping to find evidence of self-awareness. In every case, the young black bear cubs he raised reacted as if they were meeting another bear, but after sniffing the mirror and running circles around it, they seemed to conclude that they were looking at themselves. They were observed dragging their toys in front of the mirror and watching themselves at play. Kilham concluded that it would never be enough to convince most scientists, but it seemed to him a demonstration of some level of self-awareness.

Perhaps the best and most famous example of bear intelligence observed in the wild is that of the Mud Creek Grizzly in Glacier National Park. The bear had been captured twice by biologists over a two year period for research purposes. Finally the bear decided he had had enough and began to fight back. After a trap had been set with bait and cameras, he would sneak into the area, tear down the plastic strips that marked the trail to the site, set off the trap with rocks and sticks, steal the bait, gnaw on the camera until it popped open, remove the film cartridge, and smash it on a rock. This happened several times before biologists deemed it best to leave the bear alone before it started taking its frustration out on people.

At Fortress of the Bear, teamwork was often observed between Chaik and

Killisnoo. Once we hung a whole chicken from a decrepit bridge trellis high above the pool area, two feet higher than the bears could reach. Despite their best efforts, they were unable to obtain the meal. Exasperated, they sat side by side on the shore for five minutes, staring at the chicken as if working out how to get to it. Finally, with no spoken language and no visible communication between them, Chaik stood and walked around the far edge of the pool. Killisnoo stood and quietly followed him. Upon reaching the far side, Chaik rolled a stump end over end into the water until it was standing beneath the chicken. The stump was unsteady where it sat so Killisnoo put his full weight against it and held it steady while Chaik climbed up on it and retrieved the snack. They halfed it for their efforts.

On another occasion, Killisnoo inadvertently discovered how to catch fish in the pool by using the limbs of a dead Christmas tree as an impassable net or as a structure the fish would seek to take shelter in. After attempting this a few times, he figured out the limbs could act as a trap, so he moved more trees into the water. One could almost see the gears turning in his head as he gained a clearer understanding of what he was constructing. Finally, after almost creating a fully functional fish weir, he seemed to lose whatever it was he was on the verge of grasping and abandoned the project.

And people claim that captive bears offer no research value! In all truthfulness, wild bears have been studied to death; there is very little more to learn in that environment. In a captive environment, as long as they are cared for, well-fed, and given a stress-free life, a completely different side of the animal comes to the surface. This, to me, is one of the highest values of captive bears that many opponents to the practice do not see: the opportunity to witness these behaviors, to understand that they are complex and intelligent creatures, and to gain not only insight into *how* to coexist with them but to gain the *desire* to. And as we'll see in the next chapter, a very critical decision about coexistence will soon have to be made…

Chaik watching as I hang an enrichment toy from the bridge trellis.

Killisnoo being typically goofy.

Chaik eating a hunter-donated deer carcass in a snowstorm.

Chaik (left) and Killisnoo were a pleasure and a delight to watch and interact with.

# CHAPTER TWELVE:

# PEACE AND SANITY AMONG GRIZZLIES

Doug Peacock and his cat, Elk. Photo by Andrea Peacock.

I had already spent two summers in Southeastern Alaska and was just beginning my third when I read Doug Peacock's excellent *Grizzly Years* and I explicitly credit Doug's writing with helping me to define not only my love for wilderness but also my passion for grizzlies. With his words in my head, I find myself waxing philosophical whenever fortunate enough to be roaming the mountains of Montana or Alaska.

Born in Alma, Michigan, Peacock has had a lifelong love affair with wild places. Throughout two tours of duty in Vietnam, lovingly worn and wrinkled maps of Wyoming and Montana kept him sane. Each night, he would spread these maps under the stars and imagine all the wondrous things to be seen in the blank spaces unmarred by cities and towns. During the heat of combat, he held onto those images, giving himself a mental escape and perhaps something to live for as well.

Serving as a Green Beret medic, Peacock dodged bullets – some fired by his own people – lost friends, and struggled to maintain composure in the face of horror, bloodshed, and death. It was too often difficult to differentiate the good guys from the bad and Peacock at one point found himself plotting to kill a fellow officer for the murder of innocent civilians. Much to his great relief, he never had opportunity to carry out his plan.

In February 1968, Doug survived the Tet Offensive and was shattered beyond repair. "Hundreds of civilians were displaced and killed," Peacock wrote in his book *Walking It Off.* "As senior medic on A-team, I pieced together Montagnard children who had been caught in the crossfire for over a week until I began to lose my mind. I arranged to leave Vietnam then, in the middle of my second tour, as my Army enlistment was about to expire. The day I packed my bags for home, March 16, 1968, American soldiers ruthlessly murdered a minimum of 347 Vietnamese civilians forty miles to my north in a place called My Lai. The murderous potential of the political lies I witnessed during the Tet Offensive was confirmed a year later by the release of photos of the My Lai massacre. On that day, ex-Sergeant E-5 D.A. Peacock was forever shut out of heaven and earth."

Returning home, Doug found that, like many other vets, he couldn't function very well and didn't fit in with societal norms, so he hit the road, hoping to find the remote places he had spent all those days dreaming of in the war.

Stopping at a phone booth in Utah to call home and ask for money, his call was cut off by an operator requesting more change. Doug coolly produced a 12-gauge and a box of double ought from his jeep and blasted three rounds into the phone. He poured gasoline on it, struck a match, and drove away as it burst into a blaze.

Realizing the war had left him unstable and dangerous, he retreated into the Wind River Range of Wyoming, where he was temporarily incapacitated by a previously dormant strain of malaria in his system. Moving on to Yellowstone as he recovered, Doug took a dip in a hot springs to shake off the final effects of the illness.

As he soaked, a mother grizzly with two cubs approached. Having heard that grizzlies will attack anything they see (this was only a year or so after the Night of the Grizzlies incident), Peacock splashed out of the hot springs and scrambled naked up a tree to escape. He was amazed when the trio passed 40 feet away and barely spared him a glance.

Surprised by their indifference, Peacock started getting closer to grizzlies rather than running away. He took notes on their behavior, feeding habits, denning, mating, etc. Our current safety knowledge about turning your head to the side to avert an aggressive bear came about in part thanks to Doug, who observed a female grizzly using this tactic to save herself from an aggressive male that surely would have killed her otherwise. Doug tried this in some of his own encounters with great success. Now, instead of drinking himself into oblivion each night while screams and gunfire echoed through his mind, his dreams were filled with visions of bears grazing peacefully on majestic mountain slopes.

Migrating his way north to Glacier, Doug encountered his "nemesis", the most notorious bear he has ever known: an enormous, aggressive male that he referred to as the Black Grizzly.

In all of Doug's years walking with bears, he says that the Black Grizzly is the one that unnerved him the most. He personally observed the giant attacking and even killing smaller bears that invaded his mountain space.

Considering this very real threat of a violent encounter, Doug and the Black Grizzly shared a most unique relationship. No matter where Doug pitched his camp, the Black Grizzly always found it, entered the site only when Doug was away, and mauled everything that had the scent of man on it, particularly sleeping bag, clothing, and camera. The bear was sending a very clear message and Doug never took it for granted, always packing up and relocating when the grizzly told him it was time to move on.

Late one evening, Doug observed from a safe distance the Black Grizzly ferociously battling a female over territorial rights and the life of a yearling cub. The female managed to escape with her cub in tow, leaving the Black Grizzly agitated…and standing between Doug and his campsite.

With darkness swiftly approaching, Doug had no choice but to reveal himself to the monster before it had a chance to discover him by accident. The angry bear rushed straight at him, ears flat, and swatted the ground repeatedly right in Doug's face. Peacock held his ground, speaking calmly to the bear, his eyes averted. Finally the Black Grizzly mellowed and, according to Peacock, seemed to be pondering something. The bear turned away, almost sadly, and ambled off into the huckleberry bushes.

Doug quickly scrambled up the ridge to his camp and built a large fire. Half an hour later, he heard a large animal moving up the hill toward him. He quickly made a torch and could see the red glint of the Black Grizzly's eyes as he emerged from the brush and approached to within thirty feet of the blaze. The bear studied him for a long moment and then the glowing eyes blinked out when the animal turned away.

Twice more during the night, it came up the hill and approached the fire. Doug tried desperately to stay awake but soon succumbed to sleep. He woke in the morning to find himself still alive and the campsite intact.

Why hadn't the Black Grizzly just killed him? Why did it merely give messages and warnings to Doug when it readily attacked and sometimes killed other bears? Doug didn't know the answer but was grateful for the odd amount of patience and restraint exhibited. Was it possible that bears were more than indiscriminate killers?

Logging more and more encounters and gaining experience that most desk-bound scientists only dream of, Peacock saw something of a connection between the innocent civilians of Vietnam, condemned as a whole because of the actions of a few, and the way bears were regarded and treated. Perhaps by helping grizzlies, he could atone for the wrongs done in that long-ago war.

Today, Doug Peacock is considered the guru of grizzly bear conservation, was the model for George Hayduke in Edward Abbey's classic novel *The Monkeywrench Gang,* and, despite lack of formal scientific training, is considered one of the world's foremost bear experts. With one of the most intense personalities of anyone you're likely to meet (he can go from speaking gently to trees in the woods to breaking up barroom brawls with a stern command to "Shut the f__k up, I'm talking about poetry over here!"), he stands on the frontline of militant grizzly bear preservation. And right now, that kind of drive and attitude is exactly what we need if the grizzly is to have any hope of surviving the current crisis that's unfolding.

Due to increasingly warmer winter temperatures in Yellowstone, an infestation of the mountain pine beetle has spread to higher elevations where it has never before been able to survive and devastated the whitebark pine trees, whose nuts are a vital source of late-season protein for grizzly bears. In 2010, the year of the infamous Soda Butte attack, overall whitebark pine health was dramatically low. Not the lowest on record, but still a very dramatic change from 2009, which indicated one of the highest years of health that has been documented.

The details of the Soda Butte incident are murky and unclear and, like the majority of bear attacks reported by the media, the reasons why it occurred were glossed over and left unexplained. While there do seem to have been predatory aspects of the attack (one of those killed was fed upon, though it's not clear if that was the bear's intention going in or if it was an opportunistic feeding once it found itself presented with a dead body), Deborah Freele, who survived the attack and later recounted her story from a Wyoming hospital bed, said that as she screamed and resisted the bear, the animal increased the attack and did not let go and move away until Deborah went limp and played dead. Had this been predatory behavior, playing dead would have only encouraged the bear to start feeding; the fact that the bear let go of Deborah and went away indicates a defensive attack, as if something had happened to give the bear concern for the safety of her cubs.

All reports have badly misinterpreted these details, giving the impression that the bear was a predator looking for someone to eat. Somebody out there could have – and should have – clarified this bit of information.

One man was killed and fed upon, but the report is not clear about the sequence of events or about who did what when. Analyzing the incident, Doug Peacock says, "Perhaps the man fought back vigorously and bravely and she dragged him ten yards from his tent. The yearlings could have seen this – anything once dead is food to a grizzly bear – and treated the victim as they might a carcass. This sudden shift from the investigatory behavior of a grizzly around a campsite to an unexpected attack and then to treating the human victim as a food source is not unknown. This is not the same as 'predatory', though this distinction is of absolutely no consolation to the family of the victim or of any importance to the female grizzly, who was not a meat-eater. The popular press, however, voraciously fed on 'predatory' and warned, 'Beware Yellowstone bears this year; they're hungry'."

In Doug Peacock's essay "*Obama's Abandonment of the West: Global Warming, Killer Bears?*" he shows that the most interesting data from the Soda Butte Report was obtained from the analysis of isotopes in the blood, serum, and hair from the necropsy of the mother grizzly. Killed two days after the attack, it was found that, for the previous two years, she had lived on a near exclusive plant-based diet. Isotopes of carbon show the bear only ate natural plant foods, not processed sugars or agricultural syrups found in refuse. Isotopes of sulfur, which would indicate consumption of whitebark pine nuts, were not present, nor were any indications of having eaten meat. Even though it was late July, the grizzly family still wore winter coats. For that time of year, mother and young weighed in at the low end of the normal range for average bears. They were extremely malnourished.

It is well-documented in many studies that a good Yellowstone pine nut crop often results in better cub reproduction for female grizzlies because of improved general nutrition and increases a bear's odds of surviving winter hibernation.

When a female bear successfully mates, the pregnancy does not automatically take. If the female enters the den with enough stored fat and protein to support herself and young, the pregnancy begins to develop into a cub; if she has not built up sufficient fat reserves, the pregnancy terminates itself. With the loss of the whitebark, mortality rates will inevitably increase. Natural vegetation alone will not suffice to keep bears healthy.

Making matters worse, berries do not grow with abundance in Yellowstone like they do in Glacier. Cutthroat trout are threatened by lake trout, which have been illegally introduced into Yellowstone Lake. Army cutworm moths, which bears sometimes feed on in the high talus fields, are heavily influenced by pesticide spraying in the Midwest and Alberta. The wolf reintroduction program has resulted in an overpopulation that has robbed the bears of almost all winter-killed carcasses, an important source of food for grizzlies emerging in the spring.

In 2009, before the loss of whitebark pine had even reached its zenith, Doug Peacock made a grim prediction: that man-eating grizzlies, "the one in a million predatory bear, may be the Yellowstone bears of the future."

On their website, the International Grizzly Bear Study Team (IGBST) maintains a list of bear mortality/attack records in Yellowstone and whitebark pine cone reduction data from 2009 through 2011. The correlation between the two is undeniable. As previously stated, 2009 shows one of the strongest whitebark pine production years on record (though, curiously, numerous field operations in the same year show 80-88% of whitebarks already dead or dying) and the bear mortality reflects that. In going through the records, I tried to eliminate any incidents that may have involved defense of cubs or carcasses and focus only on those that were abnormal or in which bears raided campsites and residential areas in search of food. In 2009, nine such incidents were documented, with one labeled as "cause unknown, under investigation". That's actually not as high of a number as it sounds and is probably fairly average, maybe just slightly above.

The change recorded in 2010, however, is *very* dramatic. Whitebark pine production is shown to be alarmingly low with mortalities heavily increasing. A grand total of 28 incidents occurred that summer, including the Soda Butte attack, making the 9 of the previous year look infinitesimal by comparison and most were very abnormal. Five of those incidents are classified as "cause unknown, under investigation" while some others are greatly disturbing.

That October 19, a bear stalked a hunter from the elk he had just killed (apparently ignoring the carcass) and twice approached to a very close range, leaving the hunter no choice but to shoot it after the second pass. On October 23, a man was threatened by a bear that refused to go away. After attempting to scare it off with warning shots, the man blasted it with pepper spray. The bear still refused to be deterred and was killed. On October 24, a similar scenario played out. A man tried to deter an approaching bear with gunshots and bear spray but both proved to be ineffective and he had to shoot it at close range. It's very telling that all three of these abnormal pursuits occurred in October when many bears are stressed about packing on enough fat to survive the winter.

2011 shows some improvement to the health and production of the whitebark pines but still not up to where the numbers need to be and a large number of abnormal bear encounters were still reported, totaling 27, with ten of those being "unknown, under investigation". In one case, a bear who killed a hiker presumably in a surprise encounter that July was found present at the site of another death in August.

This data presents a very clear picture yet, astonishingly, the very scientists who founded this information are now either outright denying it or contend that they're still "studying the issue." Chris Servheen, Grizzly Recovery Coordinator, told me personally that there is no evidence that whitebark pine loss will negatively affect grizzlies. They're omnivores, he contends, and will find other food sources.

On that point, he's absolutely right because now those same hungry bears are roaming outside of the park boundaries into human habitations, seeking supplemental protein to replace what's been lost. Public reaction has been the standard fear and intolerance. Many are calling for sport and big game hunting regulations to be established to control what they view as an overflowing population, having no understanding of the real reason why bears are suddenly turning up in these places.

In summer 2012, Department of the Interior Secretary Ken Salazar responded to Wyoming Governor Matt Mead's request that final assessment and delisting of the Yellowstone grizzly bear population from the protections of the Endangered Species Act be completed and proposed by 2014. Salazar has since declared that the U.S. Fish and Wildlife Service and other agencies will finish their analysis of the decline of the whitebark by early 2014 and that the USFWS (U.S. Fish and Wildlife Service) will then propose the delisting.

Yellowstone's grizzlies were originally delisted by the Bush Administration in 2007, but that decision was challenged by a Montana environmental group and was overturned by a District Court in 2009. The USFWS appealed that ruling and a mixed final decision was brought down by the U.S. Court of Appeals for the Ninth Council in the fall of 2011. The decision by the Court mostly supported the delisting decision but decided that the USFWS had failed to conclusively prove that the decline in whitebark pine nuts would not harm the bears.

The USFWS was dismayed at the ruling and stated their desire was to "improve the probability of success if a new decision was challenged in court." They then developed a "new approach" to strengthen that second delisting proposal, basically to show – on paper – that the roughly 600 bears of the Yellowstone Ecosystem are actually more in the range of 1,000.

I could never be a bear biologist because it's all about politics. Science, education, and conservation are not the issues that are being focused on; rather it's about who gets the keys to the car of bear management. Chris Servheen has said that the 2007 delisting was partly to show that the Endangered Species Act was having some success and whoever can "prove" that the population is stable and growing (essentially focusing on the bears expanding their range and ignoring reasons why) and get them delisted is the one who gets to be in control. Personal political stature is the only thing most of these people are really vying for.

Having swallowed the "exploding bear population" line hook and all, Governor Mead will allow sport and big game hunting of grizzlies in Wyoming should the delisting be successful (and there's little reason to think it won't be). Mead has cited grizzlies as a "heightened threat to humans" and many locals are frothing at the mouth for an opportunity to kill one.

For bear advocates and anyone with a firm grasp on science, this is a terrifying prospect. For one, grizzly bears have one of the lowest reproductive rates of all mammals in North America. They do not reach sexual maturity until five years of age, females remain with their cubs for up to two years and, depending on environmental conditions, they may not reproduce again for three or more years after separating from previous young. With the lack of ecosystem health in Yellowstone, the reproductive rate is well below normal. Throw sport hunting into the mix and the mortality rate will very quickly exceed the birth rate, just as it did in the initial 2007 delisting. That increase in threat from humans could, based on the findings of Charlie Russell and Steve Stringham, even make the bears more defensively aggressive.

The better and more sound solution would be to let the bears move into the Wind River Range of Wyoming where winter temperatures remain cold enough to prevent the mountain pine beetle's intrusion and whitebark pines are thriving. Then let's establish travel corridors across Montana, linking Yellowstone with Glacier, where the habitat is more diverse and in much better health. This would, of course, involve getting bears over and under highways. With our technology and know-how, this is very much an attainable goal. As Doug Peacock says, "These are problems we could solve, *if* we want to."

The question is, do we want to?

**\*\*\*\***

To both Doug and I, the grizzly is the ultimate symbol of wilderness and the wild would feel that much less wild without them. Personally, I know I would have very little interest in returning to those towering mountain cathedrals of Alaska or Glacier National Park if they were not there. By their very presence alone, they inject a certain vitality and life into those places and that's part of the appeal of being out there in them.

For Doug, grizzlies mean something even more. They essentially saved his life when the traumas of Vietnam threatened to consume him. They gave him reason, purpose, peace, and sanity. They gave him a way out of his own head and they still do.

"Self-indulgence is impossible in grizzly country," Doug says. "because there's an animal out there that's far more dominant, more powerful, and you've got to pay attention. It's the one animal out there that can kill and eat you about any time it chooses, yet it almost never does. It stands as an instant lesson in humility. It stands in the face of human arrogance."

The opportunity to share space with such a large and surprisingly tolerant animal is a privilege and one that far too many people take for granted. It pains me that so many fear bears to an irrational extent. Yes, you have to be careful. You have to be cautious. You have to be respectful. You can't move down a trail in grizzly country thinking about your job or your stock portfolio or your golf game or that important business meeting you have to get to. You have to focus. You have to look, listen, hear, and smell in ways you never have before. This is not difficult; your senses are not that rusty and they will kick into gear once you get out there. The sense of life that will fill your soul is worth even the most miniscule amount of danger. I pity the thousands of people who will drive through Glacier this year without ever even getting out of their car to experience what wilderness really is.

This recent push to delist the grizzly frightens me. It frightens me and it frustrates me. People are so woefully uneducated about bears, and wildlife managers, rather than improving that education, bow to public fear and pressure to allow sport hunting of an animal that does not need it. They need tolerance, they need understanding, they need travel corridors to better habitat and they need the freedom to select that habitat for themselves. Instead, a decision is being made that could adversely affect the species to a disastrous extent. All the while, the vast majority, the voices of change, are silent on the issue. That's what infuriates me the most. I agree with Doug when he says, "We're not radical enough. We're not angry enough. We're not militant enough." His proclamation that "these are problems we could solve, *if* we want to" haunts me. I'm not so sure anymore that we do want to.

I ask Doug if this could be the beginning of the end for the grizzly, the fall of a mighty animal that defies conformity with our whims at every turn yet that grants us more mercy than we've ever granted them. His response is short, direct, and to the point: "Not if we do our job."

I hope with this book, my attempt at some form of bear literature, that I'm doing my job in giving them a voice and in making a case they can't make for themselves. In the meantime, I intend to enjoy the dusty trails, the alpine lakes, and the jagged mountain summits the grizzly calls home for however long he may remain there.

Views along the Highline Trail in Glacier National Park, some of the best grizzly country in North America. Photos by the author.

# CHAPTER THIRTEEN:

## IN DEFENSE OF POLAR BEARS

Of the three North American bears, the polar bear is the one that we know the least about. The one thing most people seem to agree on is that the polar bear is the most predatory of the main three and is the only one that will frequently hunt and kill people for food. Is this really true? Yes, there have been a few nasty encounters and some rare predatory attacks, but all the evidence suggests this is not the norm.

While bears are primarily classified as omnivores, the polar bear is the only one that is a true carnivore; a necessity due to the lack of vegetation in their icy environment. This is what leads to the common assumption that they will indiscriminately prey on man, though polar bear attack statistics are extremely low when compared to grizzlies and black bears. While it is true that this is mostly due to the fact that man and polar bear share very little space together, it could also be an indication that the polar bear isn't as aggressive as it is often thought to be.

In *The World of the Polar Bear*, Norwegian biologist Thor Larsen says that he has experienced at least a dozen attacks from polar bears, but that none were predacious in nature and all were provoked.

Russian researcher Nikita Ovsyanikov – a fascinating Charlie Russell type – lived and walked with the polar bears of Wrangel Island for a number of years and wrote an excellent, invaluable book about the experience, *Living with the White Bear*. Ovsyanikov has had over 1,500 encounters with these animals and only three of those involved bears that tried to kill him. Even then, he says that he made mistakes which provoked that aggression. In all three incidents, he was able to stop the attack by carrying a stick, behaving in a confident and aggressive manner, making himself look bigger with his parka, and using

Remarkable photos of bonding and play between a sled dog and a wild polar bear.
Photos by Norbert Rosing.

pepper spray which has a 100% success rate against polar bears due to the sensitivity of their extremely keen noses (they have been known to scent seals from up to 25 miles away).

Polar bears tend to be the most curious of all bears and will investigate anything unusual or abnormal which, when you spend most of your time on an ice flow, is almost anything that isn't frozen. They have been known to casually follow people across the ice, wander into camps, and even poke their heads into tents. With the image of a man-eater so prevalent, these bears are usually killed right away without even signs of aggression being apparent. So is the polar bear that peeks inside your tent looking for a meal or is he simply curious about what's inside?

In 1978, Naomi Uemura made the first solo trek into the North Pole and wrote about the experience in *National Geographic*. He tells the story of a polar bear that entered his camp and approached his tent. Tucked away in his sleeping bag, Uemura was sure he was doomed, particularly when the bear began shredding his tent with its claws. But, after only one sniff of the man in his bag, the bear lost interest and padded away.

In October of 2003, the nuclear submarine *USS Honolulu* surfaced near the North Pole. A lookout onboard spotted three polar bears nearby, who promptly wandered over to investigate the strange thing, showing no fear, despite having never seen such an object before.

In 1990, Nikita Ovsyanikov was reading in his cabin on Wrangel Island one night and suddenly found the structure surrounded by polar bears that were peering into the windows and pawing at the walls. Ovsyanikov simply went outside , shooed the bears away, and closed the shutters.

Charles Jonkel wrote of captured and tranquilized polar bears, saying they were as docile as black bears when approached by scientists. Many other researchers who work with the bears on the ice have said that, even when fully awake and aware, they are no more aggressive than the average North American black bear.

The gentle side of the polar bear can even be seen in a series of remarkable photographs in which one of the white bears returned to a campsite every night for a week to play, wrestle, and cuddle with a sled dog (see previous page).

Churchill, Manitoba is considered to be the polar bear capital of the world. About 1,200 or more congregate here in the fall waiting for the sea ice to form so they can move out in search of their real food: ringed seals. Despite such a large concentration of supposed man-eaters, there have only been two recorded attacks in Churchill since 1717. The locals do occasionally deal with rare problem bears, but most of them are easily deterred. In one case, a tiny woman fearlessly chased a polar bear off her porch with nothing but a broom. In another, a bear wandered into the Royal Canadian Legion Hall and the club steward shouted "You're not a member, get out!" The bear promptly turned around and left.

For those bears that do get out of hand, the town of Churchill has adopted what I think is a revolutionary idea in the field of bear management, a "polar bear jail" used to house problem bears that become a nuisance. When these bears get into trouble, they are captured and transferred to an abandoned aircraft hangar containing 28 individual cells, each about six square feet wide. Snow is pushed through the bars to supply them with water but they are given no food (polar bears typically fast on stored fat reserves during the summer just as black and grizzly bears do in the winter) and have no contact with their human captors. After serving a sentence that is often dictated by the severity of the "crime", the bears are released and usually take enough away from the experience to stay out of trouble from then on.

I think a temporary "jail" for problem bears is a fantastic idea and I wonder why something like this has not been implemented in Alaska. It's certainly a better and more humane option than bullets and, with no direct human contact, the bears will not develop a heightened aggression towards people. Instead, they would learn valuable life-saving lessons and be able to pass those lessons on to their own cubs.

## CONSERVATION STATUS

The polar bear is classified as a vulnerable species, with eight of the nineteen polar bear subpopulations in decline. This is due primarily to malnutrition or starvation owing to habitat loss. Warmer winter temperatures are causing the sea ice to melt earlier in the year, driving the bears to shore before they have built up sufficient fat reserves to survive the late summer and early fall scarcity of food. These reductions in sea ice cover also force bears to swim longer distances in search of shore, depleting their energy stores and resulting in a number of drownings. Thinner sea ice also makes it more difficult for the bears to gain access to ringed seals, leading to insufficient nourishment, lower reproductive rates in adult females, lower survival rates in cubs and juveniles, and poorer body condition in bears of all ages.

In late 2011, formation of winter ice was so late and melted so early that hungry, malnourished bears began raiding old grain stores and garbage dumps in the Hudson Bay area of Churchill. Ideally the bears should be getting onto the ice in late October or early November but this time it didn't happen until mid-January and a number of bears were found dead from starvation and even cannibalism as a result. In the spring, sea ice is melting three weeks earlier than normal and that narrow window of time the bears have to feed is expected to get smaller and smaller each year.

Polar bears burn up to one kilogram of fat for each day that they are not on the ice. They spend 150 days onshore waiting for the ice to return, leaving many bears completely emaciated by the time the sea finally freezes over again. This has led to a 22% decline in the Western Hudson Bay population and will likely result in an increase of problem bear activity and, possibly, predatory behavior.

Unfortunately, many of these dire warnings about the polar bear's future have fallen on deaf ears. Critics claim polar bear populations have increased since the 1960's, when it was estimated there were 2,000 - 5,000 individuals, to 20,000 – 25,000 today. The truth is, scientists have no idea how many bears there were in the 60's. Those estimates were based on the stories of hunters and explorers rather than scientific surveys. Polar bear researchers Steven Amstrup, Thor Larsen, and Ian Stirling all agree that any past or current estimates are all just guesses (Amstrup calls it a "WAG", a "Wild-Ass Guess") based on anecdotal evidence with no scientific support. While it can't be denied that polar bear numbers have increased due to the banning of most hunting aside from tribal practices and some very limited and expensive trophy hunts, they certainly have not quadrupled. Bottom line is, we simply *do not* know precisely how many there are or how big the population is, so getting the animal listed as threatened under the Endangered Species Act would be a smart move based on the available data.

Recently, a group of 12 polar bear experts met and discussed management options in case the ever decreasing sea ice becomes a serious threat to the polar bear's survival. Some proposed doing nothing and letting nature take its course, others pushed for rescue and rehabilitation, while still others suggested feeding the bears in a type of supplementary program. I think that is a terrific, smart, common sense idea but it's drawing a tremendous amount of controversy, particularly from the Canadian Ministry of the Environment who are still spouting the "fed bear is a dead bear" dogma.

Dr. Andrew Derocher of Polar Bears International is one of the experts who proposed the idea. He admits that it is a controversial one but not unacceptable or unheard of and is a legitimate aspect of wildlife management in some parts of the world and the United States.

Despite the criticisms the idea has gotten, I applaud it. We've already seen how supplemental feeding can be a viable option for bears during lean years to help keep them out of trouble. It would work just as well in this case and would help protect locals and tourists from the only truly carnivorous bear, even if it could only be workable as a short-term solution.

Doug Peacock believes that the fates of men and bears are mingled, our destinies intertwined, and I think he's right. Bears of any species are the proverbial canary in the coal mine. If that canary dies, do the miners stand around discussing what happened and debating what may have caused it? No, they get the hell out of the mine before they drop too.

Bears are a keystone species, which means they hold an ecosystem together. Without them, it all collapses. An environment that is healthy enough to support bears is healthy enough to support all creatures and the presence of bears is an indicator of that health. If that environment cannot support bears, then it cannot support anything, including man. The whitebark pine tree, for example, is a keystone species, one the bears rely on. Look at what's happened because of its loss. The same will happen to the polar bear when it's environment can no longer sustain its presence. Only the polar bears, unlike the grizzlies, have nowhere else to go.

As I'm writing this, President Obama has just finalized a special ruling that fails to protect polar bears from greenhouse gas emissions and oil drilling in Alaska, despite the Administration's repeated acknowledgment of the threat to this species. This new regulation, coined by some media outlets as a "Polar Bear Extinction Plan", is modeled on a previous Bush Administration measure that excluded the same activities from regulations that could prevent the bear's extinction. Without that protection, more than two-thirds of the planet's polar bears, including all individuals in Alaska, will be gone by 2050.

Maybe you don't believe in global warming or climate change. Maybe you think of it in the form of weather systems, ocean temperature cycles, natural warming/cooling periods, etc. Call it what you will but it's undeniable that something dramatic and unprecedented is happening and it's having a devastating impact on these majestic and intelligent creatures. It will have a similar impact on us and our future generations are the ones who will have to live with the decisions, good or bad, that we make right now, so it's imperative that we make the best choices that we can.

If it's not good enough to save bears for artistic, personal, or spiritual reasons, or for the humility of sharing space with them, then we should at least do it to save ourselves. If the earth reaches the point where it can no longer support them, then how much longer will it be able support us? If we're not careful and if we let these animals disappear, then our destinies really will be mingled.

And their fate will become ours.

# PART 3:
# CONCLUSION AND RESOURCES

# EPILOGUE:

## SAFE TRAVELS IN BEAR COUNTRY

Bears have a strange and inexplicable hold over us. From cartoons and children's stories to movies and a plethora of books, bears have invaded our popular culture. Kids, in particular, are fascinated by them. We all grew up with a teddy bear for companionship and for many youngsters, "bear" was the first word out of their mouths.

What is the source of this fascination, this hold they've taken on our minds and imaginations? Is it rooted in the long-ago interactions between our ancestors and the giant short-faced bears that roamed the primordial landscape? Or does it stem from the fact that there is no other animal on the North American continent that is more like us than a bear? They stand upright, have binocular vision, and cuff their young to keep them in line. Their brain patterns and cognitive abilities are equal to that of a 3 year-old child. They experience similar emotional states to our own and openly express them. The hind print of a bear closely resembles the track of a bare-footed human and the skinned carcass of a bear so closely resembles the human body that it's chilling. Maybe Doug Peacock is right; maybe we are connected in some unknowable way.

Despite being so loved and revered, they are also one of the most demonized and feared of all the creatures on this continent. The media is more than partly to blame for this. On the occasion when attacks occur, the headlines scream to the hills and back in loud, bold lettering about the horror that's transpired. You'll never see a headline proclaiming "BEAR ENCOUNTER IN YELLOWSTONE ENDS PEACEFULLY: 400 POUND GRIZZLY MINDS ITS OWN BUSINESS". These peaceful encounters, which make up more than 90% of all bear encounters per year, are not stories; they're not "entertaining" so they're not newsworthy. With media coverage focusing on attacks and seldom, if ever, breathing one word about why attacks occur and what can be done to prevent them, it's no wonder that fear and paranoia rule the day along with a disturbingly prevalent lack of knowledge about bear safety and how to conduct oneself in the woods.

Statistically, bear attacks are an aberration, almost unheard of in comparison to the more common causes of death. Automobile accidents claim roughly 42,000 lives per year (115 a day). Domesticated dogs, man's own best friend, kill 20-30 a year. Human beings kill 16,000-17,000 of their own kind per year. Bears, on average, kill 1 or 2 per year. That's still significantly less than the number of lives lost in fires, tornadoes, earthquakes, bee stings, and lightning strikes. In comparison, bears present a ridiculously small threat, one that is certainly acceptable when recreating in their backyard. In fact, you stand a greater chance of being killed in a car accident while driving to bear country than you do of being killed by a bear while walking down a trail.

In the national parks themselves, falls and drownings make up the largest number of fatalities, with exposure following closely behind. Personally, when hiking somewhere like Glacier National Park, I worry more about the effects of the sun on a hot day, bee hives, hobo spiders in the brush when I stop for a break, mountain lions (these attacks, while not quite the statistical aberration that bear attacks are, are nonetheless very rare), territorial moose, and sudden afternoon lightning storms while exposed on a mountain ridge. Even with those risks, city and urban life are much, much more dangerous than any amount of time spent outdoors in a national park.

That having been said, though, the occasional attack does occur and human lives are sometimes lost. Numbers don't mean anything to Julie Helgeson or Michele Koons or Mary Pat Mahoney (Glacier Park's other "famous" bear attack. She was drug from her tent in the Many Glacier campground on September 23, 1976) or the handfuls of others who, unfortunately, have found themselves in the wrong place at the wrong time. There is always the chance, however slight, that that could be you so it's imperative to know the reasons why bears attack and what you can do to handle such a situation should it arise.

Most bear attacks are defensive and most involve mothers protecting cubs. If a bear perceives you as a threat – if you're in an area with a lot of hunting, expect that to be a given – it will react in such a manner as to neutralize that threat.

Those bear safety pamphlets you can pick up in the national parks or almost anywhere in Alaska are a great resource but can also be full of contradictions and ambiguities. Many of these are written by park attorneys concerned about liability rather than by experts and most of them usually make one critical error: they do not differentiate between black bears and grizzly bears. Safety advice differs between the two and not knowing that can be potentially very dangerous.

## BLACK BEARS

Statistically, there have been more black bear attacks than there have been grizzly attacks. Of course, this is not because black bears are more aggressive but because their numbers are greater. This is the bear most likely to be encountered on a regular basis by readers.

Black bears tend to be shy, reclusive, and non-aggressive; certainly nowhere near as temperamental or as likely to attack as a grizzly. Unlike their larger and more volatile cousins, black bears have sharp, cat-like claws that they use to climb trees when they sense danger. Mother black bears don't attack in defense of cubs; they simply run them up a tree until the threat has passed, so encountering a black bear with young should not be the heart-in-your-throat experience that it would be with a grizzly.

Biologist Terry DeBruyn, who walked with three generations of wild black bears in Michigan, tells of observing a mother bear running her cubs up a tree with a gruff "woof". The mother then spread herself flat on the ground and disappeared into the grass, remaining that way for some time. As Terry watched from a hidden location, a couple of hikers walked past, completely unaware that bears were in the area. Mother and cubs stayed quiet for several minutes more and another hiker walked past. Five minutes later, she stood, called the cubs down, and continued on her way. This is how most encounters go. If the wind is blowing right, it will carry your scent up to two miles ahead of you as you hike. If the wind is more erratic, or if the bears are just not paying attention, then you run the risk of a surprise encounter.

The most common black bear defensive behavior you are likely to witness is nervous bluster. This is the bear's way of communicating its apprehension about the situation, not its desire to tear you limb from limb. This behavior may manifest as blowing, jaw clacking (frightening to see but still only an expression of the bear's fear), slapping the ground or an object, or, less commonly, bluff charges.

There are some experts who disagree with the theory of a bluff charge, saying that when a bear comes at you, he's working out whether to break it off or follow through all the way up until the final moment. This could be true, because your reaction in this situation will help determine the outcome. Black bears are very easily intimidated, so stand your ground, stay calm, make eye contact, and face the animal head on. If need be, hold a coat or canvas bag over your head to make yourself look bigger. If it's a hot or rainy day and you have an umbrella, pop it open in the bear's face and he'll turn tail pretty quickly.

In the unlikely event you're actually attacked by a black bear, you can safely assume the motive is predation. These freaks of nature are most always male and, unlike grizzlies, they tend to attack in broad daylight while you're away from your campsite. All the safety pamphlets tell you to play dead if you're attacked by a bear, but if it's a black bear and you have no immediate means of escape, *do not play dead!* The bear will proceed to eat you if you do. Instead, fight back with everything you've got. If you can't use a solid object as a weapon, use your fists. Go for the snout, the nose, the face, eyes, any vulnerable spot. If you have bear spray (and you should!), fend the bear off until you can get to it and use it. Bottom line, you want to convince the bear that killing and eating you is not worth the effort, that he'll expend more energy in taking you out than he would get from eating you.

As long as you follow the standard procedure of making noise as you travel and eliminating food odors in your camp, you should have no trouble at all from black bears.

## GRIZZLY BEARS

Grizzlies don't have the advantage of a black bear's razor claws. A grizzly's claws are long, dull, and rounded at the tips. These are used for excavation purposes: overturning large boulders or scooping out great mounds of earth in search of prey. This means that, unless a tree's branches are low enough and spaced just enough to permit them to use their paws to pull themselves up, they cannot climb a tree and hide. They have to tough it out on the ground, face to face with potential threats, thus they've evolved a more aggressive, standoffish attitude than the meek black bear.

Grizzlies mostly bluff too but a thin, starving bear late in the season is likely to be desperate enough to eat whatever it can find and sometimes defensive attacks can become predatory if the victim struggles or resists. On occasion, young subadult bears can be trouble. They're on their own for the first time, they're frightened, and they instinctively try to intimidate any other creature they meet. These teenagers are responsible for a large percentage of attacks on humans. In fact, it was a pair of these subadults, working together, that killed Mary Pat Mahoney in Many Glacier.

Still, it's safe to say that defensive behavior, responding to some threat perceived by the bear, is the primary cause for all aggressive encounters with a grizzly. Stay calm, stand your ground, and *do not make eye contact*. Grizzlies are not as easily intimidated as black bears and will take eye contact as a direct challenge. Lower your head and turn it to the side. This communicates submission, while standing your ground shows that you're not going to be bullied. Speak softly and calmly. This will help keep you calm and your body language will communicate that to the bear, keeping him calm. Once a grizzly feels that you're not a threat, he will back down.

In the event that you surprise a bear at close range or, God forbid, encounter a mother with cubs, absolutely do not run! This will trigger a chase response and possible predation. The fastest grizzly on record was clocked at 41 mph. The fastest human on record was clocked at 27 mph and it's probably a safe bet to say that you're nowhere near that fast. You will not outrun a bear, not even in thick brush, and even if you could get to a tree and get up it in time, a big grizzly can stand nine feet tall on its hind legs, can reach even higher than that, and will pull you out of the tree faster than you can climb it.

If you are charged and knocked to the ground, play dead. Protect your vital organs by lying flat on your stomach (no fetal position; that will leave you too exposed) and clasping your hands across the back of your neck. If the bear rolls you onto your back, keep rolling until you're on your stomach again. This is easier said than done, but stay as still and as quiet as possible. The bear will bite you, claw you, and thrash you. If you're wearing a backpack, hopefully you'll get lucky and that will take the brunt of it. Once the bear is convinced the threat is neutralized, he will back off and leave. Remain still on the ground for as long as possible until you are certain the bear is gone. Then, and only then, should you move and go for help. Stir too soon and the bear will be on you again.

A predatory grizzly should be handled the same way as a black bear. Escape if you can, use bear spray if you have it and can get to it, otherwise fight back as hard as you can, no matter how badly outmatched you may feel. The bear doesn't know that you are not meaner than he is, so convince him that you are and that you're not worth the effort.

## PREVENTING A BAD ENCOUNTER

The best bear safety advice one can give is that prevention is the best defense. Take the following precautions while in bear country and odds are you'll never even see one:

1. All safety advice says to not hike alone and always travel in groups. Very good advice but problematic if silence and solitude is what you're looking for.

I hike solo on most occasions and know dozens of others who do as well. This is your right and no one can take it from you, but know your stuff. If you're in a national park and hiking in a remote area, check with the Park Service about bear sightings and trail closures, carry bear spray and maybe even a satellite phone if you're going backcountry. Let someone know where you're going and when you expect to return.

2. Stay alert and aware; don't "speed hike" down a trail. Stop every few minutes and look around. Listen. Scent the air. Observe what other animals are doing, especially birds. Scavengers will sometimes follow predators or gather at moose carcasses, waiting for a bear to finish feeding. All of nature functions as a collective whole; if something's wrong, you'll know it. You'll feel it.

3. Make noise. When I was at Fortress of the Bear in 2010, I went for an afternoon walk in the Sitka National Historical Park, a deep forest running through an old Tlingit/Russian battle site. The salmon run was late and a bear had been seen in the park along Indian River. That day, a group of young teenagers were walking the trails, banging metal pots and pans together and shouting at the top of their lungs. No matter where you went in the park, you could not escape that horrible, irritating noise. If you're that scared, stay home! Don't ruin the wilderness experience for everyone else out there. Doug Peacock recommends moving down the trail like another animal and I agree. Many of the bears I encountered in Glacier traveled loudly, snapping sticks as they went, alerting whatever else is out there of their presence, so I snapped large sticks every few minutes or whacked them as hard as I could against the sides of trees, producing a sound so loud it echoed for ten seconds. This technique sent everything – including birds and chipmunks that had previously ignored my voice – scattering for cover.

Stephen Herrero and biologist Tom Smith conducted recent tests on wild bears in Alaska to see what sounds they would or would not respond to. The bears responded to the sound of a human voice but did not flee and bear bells were completely ignored. The only sounds that caused the bears to run were snapping sticks, clattering rocks, and low deep coughs, all sounds that would normally indicate the approach of another bear.

Lots of people swear by bear bells and more power to them, but I can never hear those things until a hiker decorated in them is right on top of me. A bear napping or preoccupied with foraging is not going to hear them any better. If conditions are windy or you're near fast-moving water, the sound disappears completely. The sound of a human voice sometimes doesn't carry that well either, though better than bear bells. Whistling is not recommended as the sound can be similar to a whistling marmot, a grizzly's natural prey.

Crack sticks, kick rocks, cough and clear your throat loudly and you'll be fine. Clap your hands and call "Hey, bear" in addition to the above if conditions are windy or if the trail runs through berry bushes, along streams, or around blind corners. Banging, crashing, and shouting runs the risk of angering a dozing bear on a daybed and that's a dangerous situation no matter how big of a group you're traveling with.

4. Don't hike with a dog. Dogs are illegal in the national parks and for good reason. Many believe that, because bears dislike dogs, hiking with a dog will keep the bears away, but it's actually more likely to result in a bad situation. If you have a dog disciplined enough to remain quiet and by your side when a bear is sighted, then you're fine. If, however, your dog is going to run after the bear, bark at it, snap at it, and run circles around it., you could find yourself in a lot of trouble. A large number of aggressive attacks have been caused by poorly trained canines that piss off a bear and then run back to their masters with *Ursus* in pursuit. The bear redirects its aggression from dog to human and the dog either ends up dead and the human badly injured or man's best friend heads for the hills while his master gets thrashed to pieces. It may be best to leave the dog at home!

5. Be mindful of colors and scents. Herrero and Smith found that bears are often attracted to bright colors, such as yellow or red and tend to ignore dark or camouflage colors. Some of these bears approached and tore down brightly-colored tents and bypassed darker ones, leading Katmai National Park rangers to adopt the usage of camouflage tents only, which they reported cut bear visitations to their campsites by half.

While testing scents, they found that bears responded to sweet, sharp odors such as perfume, fruit-scented shampoos, and citronella (an ingredient of some insect repellants). Cosmetics such as deodorant, cologne, aftershave, makeup, etc., could all be attractants as well.

Some claim that bears are attracted to menstruation while others vehemently deny it. In fact, this was one of the more widely proposed theories for why Julie Helgeson and Michele Koons were killed in 1967. A few studies have been conducted and they show that black bears, being primarily scavengers, were attracted to older, used tampons while polar bears, being pure carnivores, were actually more attracted to fresh tampons than they were to seal blubber. As far as I know, grizzlies have never been tested and maybe they should be. Until then, this subject is an open book. We really don't know the answer. Err on the side of caution and utilize the best sanitary practices possible.

6. Always carry bear spray! Some experts don't use capsaicin spray because they fear it makes the person carrying it too confident and less attentive and

they may be onto something there. The stuff is not brains in a can so don't treat it like it is. Follow all of the above rules to the letter regardless and carry bear spray in case all else fails. Research the different brands and what people are saying about them. I carry Counter Assault, which is one of the best brands out there – if not the best – and the one you're most likely to find in stores. Test fire it a time or two; get a feel for how it works and how to handle it. Read the directions thoroughly until you're comfortable with its usage. It's probably a good idea to carry at least two cans with you in case one runs out. Don't throw it in your backpack where you can't get to it. Most encounters happen quickly and unexpectedly so carry it in its belt holster or across your chest. Practice drawing it and getting the safety off.

Bear spray is a last resort. Don't use it unless all else fails and your only other option is to get mauled. Remember that the spray is a deterrent, not a repellant, so don't spray it on your clothes, sleeping bag, or tent as some unfortunates do; the scent of the residue has actually been known to attract bears.

Despite the tremendous benefits, bear spray does have a few drawbacks. If you're going to use it, be mindful of the wind; you don't want to mace yourself in that situation. There have been very few instances of bears being unfazed by bear spray, but that could be attributed to the canister being older than its projected shelf life or a lesser quality brand. Still, there is the very real risk, however unlikely, that someday a bear may only be angered by pepper spray and an attack could be provoked.

7. I don't recommend carrying a firearm. Not only are guns illegal in the parks, but they could get you into even more trouble. You have to be quite an impressive marksman to hit a small vulnerable spot on an animal built like a tank that's charging you at full speed. Bears that have had their hearts shot out of their chest and half their heads blown off have been known to live long enough to attack their shooter. If your one shot (the only shot you'll likely get) is not immediately fatal, the bear could still either maul you or run off into the woods and attack someone else. Redirected aggression as a result of previous human injury happens often so opting for bear spray over firearms may be a good idea.

8. If you're camping, prepare your food and clean your dishes 100 yards from your campsite. Change into fresh clothes and keep those with food scents away from your tent. Many frontcountry campgrounds offer bear resistant containers for food storage and most backcountry sites provide hanging poles for suspending your supplies off the ground and above a bear's reach. If neither of these are available, pack along bear proof containers or Ziploc bags to store food and keep them 100 yards or more from your tent.

SAFE TRAVELS IN BEAR COUNTRY

I highly recommend using electric fencing around your campsite. These fences are small, weigh 1-3 pounds, and are super easy to pack in and out with your gear. They typically enclose a 27ft.x27ft. area and run on 2 D-cell batteries that can supply power continuously for five weeks. The charge carried is about 6-7,000 volts with low amperage, so while it packs a shock, it won't injure the bears or you if you happen to make contact with it. I have not heard of any instances in which a bear has pressed on in its investigation of a campsite - or in which one even returned to a campsite - after touching the fence, so I feel electric fencing and bear spray should be mandatory for recreating in bear country. The UDAP website also offers an electrified mesh screen "food fence" for protecting your food and supplies, eliminating the hassle of suspending them off the ground. These are pricey, but could well be worth the investment for the serious backcountry traveler.

9. Know your bears. Don't be fooled by colorization. Black bears can be brown, cinnamon, blonde, or white. Grizzlies can be all of the above, including jet black. Learn the physical differences between the two and use that as your primary source of identification.

Some characteristical differences to watch out for: Black bears have a more elongated "Roman-nose" facial profile with long, pointed ears while grizzlies have a more dog-like dish-shaped face with short, rounded ears. The shoulder hump on a grizzly is the most notable physical difference. This is essentially an enormous mass of muscle that powers the animal's ability to excavate large boulders and mounds of dirt in search of prey. Black bears lack this large muscle, though the shoulder blades can at times create the illusion of one, particularly when the head is lowered. Study the comparisons on the next page but keep in mind that the two species can sometimes be difficult to tell apart.

10. Watch out for bear sign. Some indications that bears are, or have been, present could be trampled berry bushes, fresh tracks, scat (these are usually large, pocked with berries, and are often deposited in the middle of trails), diggings, fallen logs torn apart in search of insects, an abundance of ravens or crows that could be marking a carcass, bite or scratch marks on trees as a territory marker for other bears, or worn-down paths through thick grass. In coastal Alaska, scattered remains of salmon are good indicators that bears have been nearby.

\*\*\*\*

Biologist Mathias Breiter says that the more he learns about bears, the less sure of them he is. Sometimes I feel the same way, but I always think that if

Tall pointed
ears    No shoulder hump
Straight
face
profile

Front claw

1¹/₂" long

Short claws    **Black Bear**

Short rounded ears  Shoulder hump
Dished face
profile

Front claw

2"-4" long

Long claws    **Grizzly Bear**

some alien force were to look at us human beings from an outside perspective, they might feel the same degree of confusion. Humans are complex, intelligent beings who are molded and shaped into individual personalities through individual life experiences. Bears are so intelligent that young cubs are born almost as blank slates. They learn from their mothers how to be, how to act, what to eat, what not to eat, how to find and build a den, what's dangerous and what's not. They possess a tremendous capacity not only for learning but for re-learning, for adaptation. Individuality is the end result and just when you think you've got it all figured out, along comes some rogue bear to throw a spanner in the works. That can be very confusing if you view a bear's behavior solely from an instinctive perspective.

I never liked using the word "unpredictable" to describe bears. If they're unpredictable, imagine how downright schizophrenic we must seem to them. If a book called *Human Attacks* were written for bears, it would make us seem like the truly unpredictable ones; bloody, indiscriminate killers waiting to take out bears at every opportunity when, in reality, most people enjoy having bears around and don't want to cause them harm. The same is true of the bears themselves who mostly just want to mind their own business and – as I've said before – do a much better job of getting along with us than we do of getting along with them. That's our fault and a lack of education is the reason why.

I'm not a bear biologist, nor would I want to be. Too much politics. Too much squabbling and backstabbing, and too many restrictions on my own way of thinking. No doubt there will be some of those types who will criticize this book for being anthropomorphic. Well, of course it is! I can only interpret what I see through my own eyes just as a bear can only interpret me as another bear and respond according to the dictates of his own world. That, too, is a type of anthropomorphism. I've immersed myself in this subject long enough to feel confident that their thought patterns and emotional capabilities are not too dissimilar from ours. Many more scientists are starting to agree and I hope that trend continues.

In conclusion, I recommend reading anything and everything you can possibly stomach about bears in order to fully round out your grasp on this subject. There are plenty of resources available and I've listed a number of them in the back of this book. Some are better than others, but all have value and contain some degree of pertinent information. If you're planning on paying a visit to grizzly country, a wide diversity of information, thoughts, and opinions can only be useful to you. Then you can rest assured that you're adequately prepared for any and all possibilities.

It never ceases to amaze me the way things tend to fall into place. When I was in third or fourth grade, I was already reading on a college level and started writing my own stories not long thereafter. Hard-headed determination to go on a Caribbean cruise took me to Alaska instead when final sailings on a soon to be retired ship opened up for some of the cheapest prices in Alaska cruise history. Everything since has been a series of "coincidences" that, I believe, are not quite coincidental. This book is the culmination of it all. I don't think it will ever be counted among the classics of bear literature but I hope it will still work as an effective call to arms, shedding much-needed light on an animal that we know so very little about. The passion I've developed for bears and their secret lives is a great gift they've given to me. Now, in the dawning of what could be their darkest hour, this writing is my gift back to them.

I hope it's enough.

# NOTES AND SOURCES

## INTRODUCTION

Larry Kaniut. *Alaska Bear Tales*. Anchorage, AK.: Alaska Northwest Books, 1983.

## CHAPTER ONE: THE GREAT BEAR HOLOCAUST

Harold McCracken. *The Beast that Walks Like Man: The Lore, Legend, and History of The Grizzly Bear*. Garden City, NY.: Hanover House, 1955.

Mike Lapinski. *Grizzlies and Grizzled Old Men: A Tribute to those who Fought to Save the Great Bear*. Helena, MT.: Falcon, 2006.

## CHAPTER TWO: THE NIGHT OF THE GRIZZLIES

Jack Olsen. *Night of the Grizzlies*. Moose, WY.: Homestead Publishing, 1969.

*Glacier Park's Night of the Grizzlies*. KUFM TV/Montana PBS, 2010.

Jim Gorman. "Terror in the Night." *Backpacker Magazine* (August 2007), pages 95-103.

Author's note: "Attempting to contact Roy Ducat I was saddened to learn that he passed away in July of 2011 due to complications from heart surgery."

Thomas McNamee. *The Grizzly Bear*. New York: Knopf, 1984.

Frank C. Craighead, Jr. *Track of the Grizzly*. San Francisco: Sierra Club Books, 1979.

## CHAPTER THREE: THE PUBLIC BATTLES

David Knibb. *Grizzly Wars: The Public Fight Over the Great Bear*. Spokane, WA.: Eastern Washington University Press, 2008.

## CHAPTER FOUR: MAN'S BEST FRIEND?

"The Legacy of Bart the Bear" (video). The Vital Ground Foundation.

Author's note: "In order to avoid any such comparison to pigs, I have expressly avoided usage of the terms "boar" and "sow" to denote male and female bears throughout the course of this text."

Theodore H. Hittell. *The Adventures of James Capen Adams: Mountaineer and Grizzly Bear Hunter of California*. Taylor Trade Publishing. Original printing, 1866; reprint, 2012.

McCracken. *The Beast that Walks Like Man*. 1955.

Lapinski. *Grizzlies and Grizzled Old Men*. 2006.

Author's note: "Brown bears and grizzlies are the same species, though distinction is made between them due to the larger size of one over the other. The largest, brown bears, live along the salmon-rich Alaskan coast, while the smaller, grizzlies, inhabit the inland regions where food resources are poorer. Some scientists have drawn an invisible line along the coast to divide the two subspecies' habitat. Never mind the fact that the brown bears go up into those inland regions - crossing that non-existent line and becoming a completely different kind of bear - to hibernate, and that the grizzlies also cross that same line - themselves becoming a different subspecies in the process - to forage for leftover fish scraps on the coast. I use the distinction reluctantly."

## CHAPTER SIX: THE WAGES OF FEAR

Charlie Russell and Maureen Enns. *Grizzly Heart: Living Without Fear Among the Brown Bears of Kamchatka*. Toronto: Random House of Canada, 2002.

Charlie Russell, personal correspondence. 2010-2012.

Stephen Stringham, personal correspondence. 2010.

"Starving Bears Eat Russian Guards" *The Sydney Morning Herald*. July 25, 2008. smh.com.au

Bill Schneider. *Where the Grizzly Walks: The Future of the Great Bear*. Helena, MT.: Falcon, 2004.

Doug and Andrea Peacock. *In the Presence of Grizzlies: The Ancient Bond Between Men and Bears*. Guilford, CT.: The Lyons Press, 2009.

Kaniut. *Alaska Bear Tales*. 1983.

Jill Robinson, Annemarie Weegenaar, and Nicola Field, personal correspondence. 2012.

# CHAPTER SEVEN: THE LEGACY OF TIMOTHY TREADWELL

Timothy Treadwell and Jewel Palovak. *Among Grizzlies: Living with Wild Bears in Alaska*. New York: Ballantine, 1997.

*Grizzly Man* (documentary film). Lions Gate. Director: Werner Herzog. 2005.

Nick Jans. *The Grizzly Maze: Timothy Treadwell's Fatal Obsession with Alaskan Bears*. New York: Plume, 2006.

Charlie Russell's comments on Timothy Treadwell courtesy of Charlie and his website, Pacific Rim Grizzly Bears Co-Existence Study, cloudline.ca

"Wildlife Author Killed, Eaten by Bears He Loved." *Anchorage Daily News*. October 9, 2003. adn.com

Stephen Stringham, personal correspondence. 2013.

*Grizzly Man Diaries*. Discovery Channel/Animal Planet. 2008.

# CHAPTER SEVEN: HOPE FOR BLACK BEARS

Quotes and background info courtesy of Lynn Rogers, bear.org, and bearstudy.org.

Stephen Herrero, Terry DeBruyn, Tom Smith, Kerry Gunther, and Colleen Matt. *From the Field: Brown Bear Habituation to People – Safety, Risks, and Benefits.* Wildlife Society Bulletin, 2005.

Stephen Stringham. *Beauty Within the Beast: Kinship With Bears in the Alaskan Wilderness.* Pacific Grove, CA.: Last Post Press, 2002.

Jack Becklund. *Summers with the Bears: Six Seasons in the North Woods.* New York: Hyperion, 1999.

Benjamin Kilham and Ed Gray. *Among the Bears: Raising Orphaned Cubs in the Wild.* New York: Holt, 2003

*The Man Who Lives With Bears* (documentary). Firecracker Films, 2008.

Allen Piche, personal correspondence. 2011. Also citings from his website thebeardude.net.

## CHAPTER NINE: SEEK THE BLACK BEAR CUB

"Black Bear Cub Finds New Life, Friends in Sitka." *Daily Sitka Sentinel.* May 20, 2010.

Les Kinnear, personal conversation. 2010.

## CHAPTER TEN: LEARNING TO TALK BEAR

Stephen Stringham. *When Bears Whisper, Do You Listen?* Soldotna, AK.: WildWatch Press, 2009.

## CHAPTER ELEVEN: BEAR INTELLIGENCE

Stringham. *Beauty Within the Beast.* 2002.

Else Poulsen. *Smiling Bears: A Zookeeper Explores the Behavior and Emotional Lives of Bears.* Vancouver, BC.: Greystone Books, 2009.

Kaniut. *Alaska Bear Tales.* 1983.

Stephen Herrero. *Bear Attacks: Their Causes and Avoidance.* New York: Lyons and Burfod, 1985; revised and updated, 2002.

Kilham. *Among the Bears.* 2002.

Roland Cheek. *Learning to Talk Bear: So Bears Can Listen.* Columbia Falls, MT.: Skyline Publishing, 1997.

Les Kinnear, personal conversation, 2011.

## CHAPTER TWELVE: PEACE AND SANITY AMONG GRIZZLIES

Doug Peacock. *Walking It Off: A Veteran's Chronicle of War and Wilderness.* Spokane, WA.: Eastern Washington University Press, 2005.

Doug Peacock. *Grizzly Years: In Search of the American Wilderness.* New York: Holt, 1990.

Lapinski. *Grizzlies and Grizzled Old Men.* 2006.

Peacock. *In the Presence of Grizzlies.* 2009.

Doug Peacock. *Obama's Abandonment of the West: Global Warming, Killer Bears?* counterpunch.org, 9/23/10.

Interagency Grizzly Bear Study Team annual reports.

Chris Servheen, personal correspondence. 2012.

Democracy Now: Doug and Andrea Peacock, 2009.

Doug Peacock, personal correspondence. 2011.

## CHAPTER THIRTEEN: IN DEFENSE OF POLAR BEARS

Thor Larsen. *The World of the Polar Bear.* London: Hamlyn, 1978.

Nikita Ovsyanikov. *Polar Bears: Living with the White Bear.* Minneapolis, MN.: Voyageur Press, 1996.

Naomi Uemura. "Solo to the Pole." *National Geographic Magazine,* September 1978.

Richard Ellis. *On Thin Ice: The Changing World of the Polar Bear.* New York: Vintage, 2010.

Peter Dykstra. "Magic Number: A sketchy "fact" about polar bears keeps going…and going…and going." *SEJournal,* Summer 2008.

Polar Bears International: polarbearsinternational.org

"New Report Suggests Feeding Polar Bears: Lists ways to save species should climate change threaten its survival." *CBC News.* 2013.

## EPILOGUE: SAFE TRAVELS IN BEAR COUNTRY

Peacock. *In the Presence of Grizzlies.* 2009.

CDC website.

Terry DeBruyn. *Walking with Bears: One Man's Relationship with Three Generations of Wild Bears.* Guilford, CT.: The Lyons Press, 1999.

Kaniut. *Alaska Bear Tales.* 1983, page 13.

Schneider. *Where the Grizzly Walks.* 2004.

UDAP website.

# BIBLIOGRAPHY

For those interested in pursuing their own bear education, there are more than a few options to choose from. I've read somewhere in the range of 5 or 6 dozen books on the topic and that's probably not even a third of the resources that are available. I'm not going to try listing them all; just those that are the most informative or that may be of greatest interest to the reader. Aside from a few exceptions, I've avoided gratuitous attack books unless they provide analysis of why such incidents occurred.

Anderson, Casey. *The Story of Brutus*. New York: Pegasus, 2010. Aside from some harrowing wilderness experiences, Anderson's first book is mostly focused on the grizzlies of North America and the relationship he has with orphaned bear Brutus. He recounts a couple of remarkable stories in which Brutus seems to shed real tears while being cared for by Casey.

Becklund, Jack. *Summers with the Bears*. New York: Hyperion, 1999.

Breiter, Mathias. *Bears: A Year in the Life*. Buffalo, NY.: Firefly, 2005.

Breiter, Mathias. *The Bears of Katmai*. Ontario: BriterView Publishing, 2008. One of the most stunning and spectacular photo books I've ever seen, particularly Breiter's underwater shots of a grizzly swimming and fishing for salmon. An excellent coffee table book!

Busch, Robert H. *The Grizzly Almanac: A Fully Illustrated Natural and Cultural History of America's Great Bear*. Guilford, CT.: The Lyons Press, 2004.

Cheek, Roland. *Learning to Talk Bear*. Columbia Falls, MT.: Skyline Publishing, 1997. One of the best outdoor writers working today with keen insights into the world of grizzlies. You'll feel as though you're right beside him in the mountains of Glacier National Park.

Cheek, Roland. *Chocolate Legs: Sweet Mother, Savage Killer?* Columbia Falls, MT.: Skyline Publishing, 2001. Analyzing the most recent, and somewhat suspect, bear attack in Glacier National Park in 1998.

Craighead Jr., Frank C. *Track of the Grizzly*. San Francisco: Sierra Club Books, 1979. Of particular note here is the final chapter, in which Frank describes the confrontations that ensued with the Yellowstone Park Service after Frank and his brother John criticized their bear management practices and proposed better and more workable strategies.

Debruyn, Terry. *Walking with Bears*. Guilford, CT.: The Lyons Press, 1999.

Dufresne, Frank. *No Room for Bears*. Anchorage, AK.: Alaska Northwest Books, 1991; first printing, 1965.

Ellis, Richard. *On Thin Ice*. New York: Vintage, 2010.

Gailus, Jeff. *The Grizzly Manifesto*. Vancouver, BC.: RMB, 2010.

Herrero, Stephen. *Bear Attacks: Their Causes and Avoidance*. New York: Lyons and Burford, 1985; revised and updated, 2002.

Hunter, Linda Jo. *Lonesome for Bears*. Guilford, CT.: The Lyons Press, 2008.

Jans, Nick. *The Grizzly Maze*. New York: Plume, 2006.

Kaniut, Larry. *Alaska Bear Tales*. Anchorage, AK.: Alaska Northwest Books, 1983.

Kaniut, Larry. *More Alaska Bear Tales*. Anchorage, AK.: Alaska Northwest Books, 1989.

Kilham, Benjamin and Ed Gray. *Among the Bears*. New York: Holt, 2003.

Knibb, David. *Grizzly Wars*. Spokane, WA.: Eastern Washington University Press, 2008.

Lapinski, Mike. *Grizzlies and Grizzled Old Men*. Helena, MT.: Falcon, 2006.

McCracken, Harold. *The Beast that Walks Like Man*. Garden City, NY: Hanover House, 1955.

McMillion, Scott. *Mark of the Grizzly*. Guilford, CT.: The Lyons Press, 1998; revised and updated, 2011.

McNamee, Thomas. *The Grizzly Bear*. New York: Knopf, 1984.

Morgan, Chris. *Bears of the Last Frontier: The Adventure of a Lifetime Among Alaska's Black, Grizzly, and Polar Bears*. New York: Stewart, Tabori and Chang, 2011. Great companion piece to the PBS Nature documentary of the same name. Beautiful photos!

Murray, John A. (editor). *The Great Bear: Contemporary Writings on the Grizzly*. Anchorage, AK.: Alaska Northwest Books, 1992. A fascinating compilation of essays on the grizzly bear and its place in nature, including Edward Abbey, Doug Peacock, Aldo Leopold, Frank Craighead, and others.

Neal, Chuck. *Grizzlies in the Mist*. Moose, WY.: Homestead Publishing, 2003.

Olsen, Jack. *Night of the Grizzlies*. Moose, WY.: Homestead Publishing, 1969.

Ovsyanikov, Nikita. *Polar Bears: Living with the White Bear*. Minneapolis, MN.: Voyageur Press, 1996.

Peacock, Doug. *Grizzly Years*. New York: Holt, 1990.

Peacock, Doug. *Walking It Off*. Spokane, WA.: Eastern Washington University Press, 2005.

Peacock, Doug and Andrea. *The Essential Grizzly: The Mingled Fates of Men and Bears*. Guilford, CT.: The Lyons Press, 2006; reprinted as *In The Presence of Grizzlies: The Ancient Bond between Men and Bears* in 2009.

143

Peacock, Doug. *In the Shadow of the Sabretooth: A Renegade Naturalist Considers Global Warming, the First Americans, and the Terrible Beats of the Pleistocene.* Oakland, CA.: AK Press, 2013.

Poulsen, Else. *Smiling Bears.* Vancouver, BC.: Greystone Books, 2009.

Russell, Andy. *Grizzly Country.* New York: The Lyons Press, 1967. Written by Charlie Russell's father, who helped shape Charlie's ideas about bears.

Russell, Charlie. *Spirit Bear.* Toronto: Key Porter Book, 1994. Russell's peaceful experiences with the docile bears of British Columbia's Queen Charlotte Island – bears who had virtually no contact with humans – ultimately paved the way for his experiment in Kamchatka.

Russell, Charlie and Maureen Enns. *Grizzly Heart.* Toronto: Random House of Canada, 2002. Still the best!

Russell, Charlie and Maureen Enns. *Grizzly Seasons.* Buffalo, NY.: Firefly, 2003. An impressive, coffee-table photo book companion to *Grizzly Heart*.

Schneider, Bill. *Where the Grizzly Walks.* Helena, MT.: Falcon, 2004.

Shepard, Paul and Barry Sanders. *The Sacred Paw: The Bear in Nature, Myth, and Literature.* New York: Arkana, 1985.

Smith, Dave. *Backcountry Bear Basics: The Definitive Guide to Avoiding Unpleasant Encounters.* Seattle, WA.: The Mountaineers Books, 2006.

Stirling, Ian. *Polar Bears: A Natural History of a Threatened Species.* Fitzhenry & Whiteside: Ontario, 2011.

Stringham, Stephen. *Beauty Within the Beast.* Pacific Grove, CA.: Last Post Press, 2002.

Stringham, Stephen. *Bear Viewing in Alaska.* Helena, MT.: Falcon Guides, 2007.

Stringham, Stephen. *Alaska Magnum Bear Safety Manual.* Soldotna, AK.: WildWatch Publications, 2008.

Stringham, Stephen. *When Bears Whisper, Do You Listen?* Soldotna, AK.: WildWatch Publications, 2009.

Stringham, Stephen. *Ghost Grizzlies and Other Rare Bruins.* Soldotna, AK.: WildWatch Publications, 2010.

Stringham, Stephen. *The Language of Bears.* Soldotna, AK.: WildWatch Publications, 2013.

Tighem, Kevin Van. *Bears Without Fear.* Calgary, AB.: Rocky Mountain Books, 2013.

Treadwell, Timothy and Jewel Palovak. *Among Grizzlies.* New York: Ballantine, 1997.

Wright, William H. *The Grizzly Bear.* Lincoln, NB.: University of Nebraska Press, 1977; originally printed 1909.


## ARTICLES AND PAPERS

Chadwick, Douglas H. "How Many Grizzlies are Enough?" *National Geographic.* nationalgeographic.com, 2/21/12.

Gorman, Jim. "Terror in the Night." *Backpacker Magazine* (August 2007), pages 95-103. The first time in 40 years that many of the survivors of the "Night of the Grizzlies" had publicly spoken of the incident.

Herrero, Stephen; Terry Debruyn, Tom Smith, Kerry Gunther and Colleen Matt. *From the Field: Brown Bear Habituation to People – Safety, Risks and Benefits.* Wildlife Society Bulletin, 2005.

Jans, Nick. "The Wrong Bear." *Alaska Magazine* (October 2011), pages 8-10.

Luczycki, Rebecca. "Last Chance – Viewing Polar Bears at Kaktovic is the Trip of a Lifetime – For Now." *Alaska Magazine* (February 2010), pages 33-35.

Nunnally, Chris. "The Bear Attacks of 1967: Remembering Michele Koons and Julie Helgeson." *The Inside Trail* (Spring 2013). Minneapolis, MN: The Glacier Park Foundation. Also available as an Amazon Kindle download under the title "Night of the Grizzlies, 45 Years Later" with a bonus essay "Brown Bear's World: Fortress of the Bear."

Nunnally, Chris "Brown Bear Summer." *Alaska Magazine* (July/August 2013).

Rogers, Lynn. "Does Diversionary Feeding Create Nuisance Bears and Jeopardize Public Safety?" *Human-Wildlife Interactions.* 5(2): 287-295.

Rogers, Lynn. "How Dangerous are Black Bears? Can We Coexist with Them?" Take Action 5(1): S. Reprinted in *The North Bearing News* (North American Bear Center publication) 1(1): 1-2. December 1996. Reprinted in *The Botany Bulletin* (North Carolina), December 2000.

Peacock, Doug. *Obama's Abandonment of the West: Global Warming, Killer Bears?* counterpunch.org, 9/23/10.

Peacock, Doug. *The Fate of the Yellowstone Grizzly.* Counterpunch.org, 5/6/09.

Smith, Tom. "Protecting Your Camp: Electric Fencing." Alaska Science Center.

Stringham, Stephen. "What Captive Bears Can Teach Us." Bear-viewing-in-alaska.info.

## DOCUMENTARIES

*Bears of the Last Frontier.* PBS Nature, 2011. Three-part companion series to Chris Morgan's book of the same name. Both of these are a precursor to Morgan's upcoming film *Beartrek.*

*Bearwalker of the Northwoods.* BBC Natural World Series, 2009. Excellent and well-made film about Lynn Rogers and his work with the wild black bears of Minnesota. Available through bear.org.

*The Edge of Eden: Living with Grizzlies.* River Road Films, 2007. Wonderful 90 minute documentary focusing on Charlie Russell's work in Kamchatka post *Grizzly Heart.* Filmed and edited by Charlie's friends Jeff and Sue Turner.

*Glacier Park's Night of the Grizzlies*. KUFM TV/Montana PBS, 2010. A sensitive, well-made, and heartbreaking retelling of the 1967 Night of the Grizzlies tragedy. Many of the survivors interviewed herein are speaking publicly about it for the first time. A worthy companion piece to Jack Olsen's excellent book, this film never fails to move me. Narrated by actor and Montana native J.K. Simmons.

*Grizzly Man*. Lions Gate. Director: Werner Herzog. 2005. One man's interpretation of Timothy Treadwell and his mindset. Critically lauded but heavily criticized by those who knew Treadwell personally.

*Grizzly Man Diaries*. Discovery Channel/Animal Planet, 2008. A fascinating eight-part miniseries exploring the life and work of Timothy Treadwell through his own journal entries and the lens of his camera. No skillful editing here, so a very different world than the one constructed by Herzog and well worth the time for anyone intrigued by that movie.

*Growing Up Grizzly*. Live/Artisan, 2001. A film about the work of Doug Seus. It begins shortly after the death of Bart the Bear and the arrival of Honey Bump and Little Bart. The Seus family is depicted overcoming the hurdles of acclimating the cubs to human life and preparing them for a career in front of the cameras. Fascinating stuff but can be difficult to find a copy. Hosted by Brad Pitt.

*Growing Up Grizzly 2*. Arden Entertainment, 2003. This sequel picks up two years after the first. Honey Bump and Little Bart have gotten older and bigger so the camera crew drops in to see how well they've adjusted to their new life. Hosted by Jennifer Aniston. As far as I know, it's only available under the title *Real Grizzly* through the Vital Ground Foundation. Vitalground.org.

*The Man who Lives with Bears*. Firecracker Films, 2008. Very hard to find documentary about Charlie Vandergaw who fed wild black and grizzly bears at his remote Alaskan cabin for over 20 years without once having an aggressive or harmful encounter. Occasionally it pops up in repeats on Animal Planet.

*The Man who walks with Bears*. Tremendous Entertainment, 2001. An older, but no less riveting documentary about the work of Lynn Rogers as he attempts to overcome the public's dogmatic beliefs about black bear behavior. Narrated by Mark Hamill.

*Polar Bear Alcatraz.* TUTM Entertainment, 2009. Follows the adventures of Russian scientist Nikita Ovsyanikov living and working alongside a large population of polar bears on desolate Wrangel Island.

*Stranger Among Bears.* Firecracker Films, 2009. A six-part miniseries focusing further on Charlie Vandergaw and the wild bears he interacts with. Virtually impossible to find.

*Walking with Giants: The Grizzlies of Siberia.* PBS Nature, WNET/Thirteen, 1999. An older documentary about Charlie Russell and Maureen Enns set during the events recounted in *Grizzly Heart.* Not as good a presentation as *The Edge of Eden* and Charlie tells some amusing stories in his book about why.

7118090R00086

Made in the USA
San Bernardino, CA
22 December 2013